American University Studies

Series VII
Theology and Religion

Vol. 8

PETER LANG
Berne · Frankfurt am Main

Orige

A

New York

Antonia Tripolitis

Origen

A Critical Reading

PETER LANG
New York · Berne · Frankfurt am Main

Library of Congress Cataloging in Publication Data

Tripolitis, Antonia:
  Origen: A Critical Reading.

  (American University Studies.   Series VII, Theology
and Religion; vol. 8)
    Bibliography: p.
    Includes index.
    1. Origen – Criticism and Interpretation.   I. Title.
II. Series: American University Studies.   Series VII,
Theology and Religion; v. 8.
BR65.068T75   1985   230'.13'0924   85-9949
ISBN 0-8204-0213-3
ISSN 0740-0446

CIP-Kurztitelaufnahme der Deutschen Bibliothek

Tripolitis, Antonia:
Origen: A Crit. Reading / Antonia Tripolitis.
– New York; Berne; Frankfurt am Main: Lang,
1985.
    (American University Studies: Ser. 7, Theology
    and Religion; Vol. 8)
    ISBN 0-8204-0213-3

NE: American University Studies / 07

© Peter Lang Publishing, Inc., New York 1985

Printed by Lang Druck, Inc., Liebefeld/Berne (Switzerland)

To the loving memory of my Mother

Contents

Preface

The purpose of this study is to present the main aspects of Origen's thoughts in a critical analytical manner as best as can be ascertained from his extant writings. Origen's works used in the study include the known Greek texts and fragments and Latin versions or translations where they support the known Greek texts. In addition, the study attempts to present Origen's view within the framework of his background and the times and environment in which he wrote. It does not attempt to discuss in detail nor to debate the controversies which were waged and continue to be waged over certain of his doctrines.

Origen is an enigmatic figure, his works are difficult to analyze and understand. This difficulty is due to the fact that his writings are of a very diverse and complex nature. Some are sophisticated philosophical treatises and others are totally biblical. Moreover, the major portion of his works has been lost and many of his important treatises, and in particular his most controversial one, *First Principles*, survive in questionable fourth-century Latin translations. Even much of his extant works in Greek are very obscure and difficult to interpret. In particular, the complex nature of his work and his pioneering speculations in his explication of the Christian views has perplexed many interpreters of his work both in his day and through the centuries to the present time. During his lifetime his teachings gave rise to much widespread questioning, and he was very often misrepresented. He was highly praised by some members of the Church and considered a heretic by others. This ambiguous view of Origen has persisted to the present day, and questions debated during his lifetime continue to be asked today. Thus, the task of presenting a truly critical and impartial interpretation of his works is made exceedingly difficult.

I wish to thank the Rutgers University Research Council for their generous support in the preparation of the manuscript.

Chronology

There does not exist a complete, accurate biography of Origen. Some facts about his life and the dates of many of his works, especially the works that have been lost, are not known. The details of his life that are known are derived primarily from Eusebius' *Ecclesiastical History*, which was written in the fourth century A.D. However, Eusebius' information is not complete. There is no account of Origen's most critical period, his retirement from Alexandria in A.D. 232. The writings of Origen himself offer very few details about the circumstances of his life. Any biographical information derived from them is usually inferred. Thus, the biographical details about Origen are not absolutely certain in many instances, and many dates given below are approximate, within a few years.

A.D. 183/185 Origen born in Egypt, probably Alexandria.

202/203 Designated the head of the famous school of sacred science at Alexandria, Egypt, by the bishop of that city, Demetrius.

214 Visited Arabia to instruct the Roman governor there at the latter's request.

214/215 Began the study of the Hexapla.

215 Took refuge at Caesarea, Palestine, during the pillaging of Alexandria by Emperor Caracalla.

220/223 Wrote *First Principles*.

226/231 Began the *Commentary on the Gospel of St. John*, Books I–V.

229/230 Went to Athens at the invitation of the

Church of Greece to settle certain ecclesiastical, doctrinal questions.

Wrote the treatise on the *Resurrection* in Alexandria.

230 Ordained as presbyter in Caesarea, Palestine, by his two episcopal friends, Theoctistus, Bishop of Caesarea and Alexander, Bishop of Jerusalem.

230/231 Bishop Demetrius recalled Origen to Alexandria. He then summoned a synod of bishops and presbyters which relieved Origen of his teaching duties in Alexandria, excommunicated him from that church and asked him to leave the city.

231 Bishop Demetrius called a second synod of bishops and deposed Origen from the priesthood.

231/232 Wrote *Miscellanies*.

232 Origen returned to Alexandria after the death of Bishop Demetrius. Heraclas, Demetrius' successor repeated the excommunication and Origen left Alexandria never to return.

232/238 Founded the school of theology at Caesarea, Palestine.

232/238 Completed the *Commentary on the Gospel of St. John*, Books VI–XXXIII.

233/236 Wrote *On Prayer*.

235 Wrote *Exhortation to Martyrdom*.

237/243 Composed the letter to his pupil Gregory Thaumaturgus.

240 Wrote the letter to Africanus and the *Commentary on the Song of Songs*.

243 Wrote the *Commentary on the Epistle to the Romans*.

244 Went to Arabia to convert Bishop Beryllus of Bostra from his heretical views on the Incarnation.

1
Origen and His Times

I. Introduction

Origen was a product of the eclectic intellectual environment of the Egyptian metropolis of Alexandria in the third century A.D. Alexandria, founded in 331–32 B.C. by Alexander the Great, gave birth to Hellenism; a civilization which was created through the meeting and fusion of East and West—Oriental, Egyptian and Greek cultures. The comingling of these three disparate cultural traditions produced a civilization which was influential in a number of directions, and one which helped to give both the Western and Eastern world the configuration of their cultures.

The city of Alexandria boasted a brilliant intellectual environment, centered around a library containing approximately 500,000 volumes adjoined by various lecture halls in which were held continuous philosophical discussions. It was in the city of Alexandria that Jewish Hellenistic literature and thought began and developed. There, in the first century A.D., the Jewish Hellenistic philosopher, Philo, attempted in numerous works written in Greek to correlate biblical revelation and Greek philosophy. Employing the popular method of the time, allegorical interpretation, Philo was able to bring the Scriptures into conformity with Greek philosophical thought. Interpreting the Scriptures allegorically, and in particular the Pentateuch, Philo was able to successfully find in the Scriptures the contemporary Greek philosophical views which could serve his purpose—to reconcile Hebrew theology with Greek Philosophy while reserving intact the observance of the Law.

Philo's thought was influenced by the Platonic tradition of that time—an eclectic Platonism which had absorbed the teaching of Aristotle, the Stoics, and the Neo-Pythagoreans. It was to this intellectual environment that Christianity arrived and mingled at the end of the first century A.D. As a result, there developed among the Christian thinkers a strong interest in philosophical speculation and the metaphysical investigation of the Christian faith, in an attempt to adapt the eclectic Platonism of the time to the requirements of Christian theology. To accomplish this, the Alexandrian Christian thinkers, similar to the Hellenistic Jewish philosopher Philo, adopted the allegorical method of interpretation. By interpreting the Scriptures allegorically, the Christian thinkers of Alexandria were able to find a deeper meaning and significance in the Gospel, within which could also be found the theses and concepts of Greek philosophy. One of the principal and most influential Christian thinkers of the eclectic, cultural and intellectual environment of Alexandria was Origen.

II. His Life

Origen was born in Egypt, probably in Alexandria, about A.D. 183–185. The principal source of his early life is derived from a biographical sketch found in the sixth book of Eusebius' *Ecclesiastical History*.[1] Eusebius claims to have derived the information found in this sketch from official documents, letters of Origen which he had collected and information received from individuals who were acquainted with Origen (H.E. VI. 2:1; 33; 36:3). According to this account, Origen, whose surname was Adamantios, "Man of Steel", was raised as a Christian and was educated in the Scriptures as well as in all the branches of secular learning. In fact, it is believed that he attended the lectures of Ammonius Saccas, who laid the foundation for the NeoPlatonic school (H.E. VI. 2:19). When Origen was not quite seventeen, his father, Leonides, was martyred during the persecution of Septimus Severus in A.D. 202/3. His father's property was confiscated by the State and he, his mother and six younger brothers were left in poverty with Origen as the sole support (H.E. VI. 2:15). In the following year, Demetrius, Bishop of Alexandria, designated him the head of the Church's catechetical school. Origen maintained this post for years, and attracted numerous students to the school from both the pagan schools of philosophy and the heretical circles by his erudite teaching and the stern ascetic simplicity of his mode of life (H.E. VI. 3:7).

Between the years 211 and 218, Origen spent much of his time journeying throughout Magna Graecia, Asia Minor and the Near East. About A.D. 212, during the episcopate of Zephyrinus, Origen visited Rome to meet the members and teachers of the Church there (H.E. VI. 14:10). While in Rome, according to Jerome, he met and heard the Roman presbyter Hippolytus preach (De vir illustr. 61). Sometime in late A.D. 214, he visited Arabia to confer with the Roman governor there at the latter's invitation (H.E. VI. 19). In A.D. 215, the Emperor Caracalla invaded Alexandria, pillaged the city and ordered a full scale persecution of the Christians. At this time, Origen left Alexandria and went to Caesarea in Palestine. There, at the request of Theoctistus, Bishop of Caesarea and Alexander, Bishop of Jerusalem, he preached and lectured to the congregation on the Scriptures. Since he was not an ordained member of the Church, Bishop Demetrius strongly disapproved of this procedure, which he claimed was unprecedented, and immediately recalled him to Alexandria (Ibid.).

Shortly after his return to Alexandria, from circa 218 to 230, Origen devoted himself almost entirely to literary activities. It was at this time that he began his work on the commentaries on the Holy Scriptures (H.E. VI. 23). His literary activity was greatly aided and encouraged by the wealthy Alexandrian, Ambrose, a Valentinian Gnostic whom Origen had converted to Christianity (H.E. VI. 18). Ambrose, according to Eusebius, provided Origen with seven stenographers and copyists and several girls skilled in penmanship (H.E. VI. 23). Among the works that Origen wrote under Ambrose's auspices are the Hexapla, or six-fold Bible, a critical text of the Old Testament;

3

his *Commentary on John;* and the *Contra Celsum,* or *Against Celsus,* a refutation of Celsus' work *The True Doctrine* which the pagan philosopher Celsus wrote against Christianity about A.D. 178 (Cels. pref. 1).

About A.D. 230, at the invitation of the leaders of the Church of Greece, Origen went to Athens to settle certain doctrinal questions affecting the Church. He travelled to Athens via Caesarea. While in Caesarea, he was ordained presbyter of the Church by the bishops of Caesarea and Jerusalem, Theoctistus and Alexander (H.E. VI. 8:4; 23). The action of the Palestinian bishops, coupled, it is thought, with Origen's increasing popularity, angered Bishop Demetrius (H.E. VI. 8). When Origen returned to Alexandria in A.D. 231, Demetrius convened a synod of bishops and presbyters which deposed him from the priesthood and excommunicated him from the Church of Alexandria. As a result of the synods decision, Origen went to Caesarea in Palestine. There, for the next twenty years until his death, under the auspices of the bishops of Palestine, he established a catechetical school similar to that at Alexandria, and continued his theological teaching. With the aid of Ambrose, he continued to pursue his literary activity (H.E. VI. 26, 27). In Caesarea, as in Alexandria, Origen continued to attract numerous students, among which were included a number of future Church leaders. One of his students, Gregory Thaumaturgus, or the Wonderworker, who later became bishop of Pontus, describes Origen's teaching and influence on the students at the school of Caesarea in his *Farewell Address.*[2] In this address, delivered upon the completion of his studies at Caesarea, Gregory vividly recounts Origen's scholarly attainments, his interest in and friendship for his students and their academic and personal development, his abilities as a teacher, his humaneness as an individual, and his devotion and piety as a Christian. This narrative is the most descriptive account remaining of Origen's method of instruction and his personal character and might be considered the best introduction to the study of Origen's works.

During his later life at Caesarea, Origen made a visit to Athens and two trips to Arabia. He visited Athens and remained there for a period of time to work on his commentaries (H.E. VI. 32). In A.D. 244, he went to Arabia to convert Bishop Beryllus of Bostra from his false views on the incarnation (H.E. VI. 33). Shortly thereafter, he returned to Arabia. This time it was to convince Bishop Beryllus of the error of his views concerning the human soul and the Resurrection (H.E. VI. 37).

In A.D. 249/250, during the Decian persecution, Origen was imprisoned and tortured (H.E. VI. 39:5). He was released from prison in A.D. 251, after the death of Decius. However, the hardships endured in prison had weakened him considerably, and he died in A.D. 253, in Tyre, at the age of seventy (H.E. VII. 1). Despite his popularity and influence in Palestine, Athens and Arabia, the Church of Alexandria, even after the death of Bishop Demetrius, appears to have made no effort to revoke Origen's excommunication.

III. The Church

Nothing is known of the events of the Christian Church in Egypt until about A.D. 180. At that time, according to Eusebius, Pantaenus, a Stoic philosopher who had converted to Christianity, came to Alexandria. It was, apparently, he who organized the catechetical school in Alexandria, became its director, and remained in charge of the institution until his death sometime shortly before A.D. 200 (H.E. V. 10:1–4). No further information is known about Pantaenus or of the origins of the catechetical school. Moreover, it is not known if Pantaenus committed any of his thoughts and teachings to writing, since there are none extant. However, Eusebius (H.E. V. 10) and his pupil and successor to the directorship of the school, Clement of Alexandria (Strom. I. 1:11) claim that he was a very successful teacher and had won universal acclaim.

Initially, the catechetical school was not a "school" as such, but a voluntary, unofficial group of scholars interested in the study and exposition of the Scriptures. Its aim was to prepare the catechumens for service to the Church. The school appears to have evolved to meet the needs of a growing Church within a cosmopolitan educated community. By the late second, early third century, under the leadership first of Clement of Alexandria and then of Origen who succeeded him, the school had developed into a center of Christian scholarship, a center of sacred science comparable in academic quality to the best pagan philosophical schools. Under Origen's tutelage, it was attended by adherents of all philosophies and religions; it was open to all who were interested in the theology of the Christian Church. The school was under the jurisdiction of the head of the Alexandrian church, the bishop. It was he who appointed its director and supervised the instruction.

According to Origen, the office of the teacher or instructor of the school was one of importance, if not the most important, in the spiritual life of the Christian community. It was the teacher who by his spiritual knowledge can transmit and teach others the truths about the Christian faith (Hom. Lev. VI. 6).[3] He considered the teaching and exposition of the Scriptures of greater significance than the celebration of the liturgical functions (Hom. Lev. V. 3; VI. 6; IX. 1; XII. 7). The latter, since they are visible signs or rites, he regarded as mere shadows of the spiritual things which they represented. Origen considered the position of the spiritual teacher comparable to that of the priest or presbyter and it demanded similar virtues.

There existed two distinct hierarchies in the Church during Origen's time. These included the official clerical offices of the bishop, priest and deacon, and the office of the teacher or instructor. Each group concerned itself with different aspects of the Church's life. The official clergy emphasized the sacred rites by which salvation might be gained; the teachers stressed the faith which the Church taught, or the interpretation of Scripture. Origen's writings clearly indicate that he favored the latter group, and was himself a member of it. In fact, he was often quite critical of the clerical hierarchy and their way of life (Comm. Matt. XVI. 8, 22). In addition, he felt that many of them were not men of learning and thus not capable of teaching others the truth about the Christian faith (Hom. Lev. VI. 6). The Church was, to him, a school which should continuously seek to elevate its members to higher degrees of spiritual knowledge through the teaching and exposition of the Scriptures.

In his writings, Origen gives considerable information on the main religious traditions of the time. They included the sacraments of Baptism and the Eucharist or Holy Communion and prayer. As with all liturgical functions, Origen considered the sacraments, although essential, as only allegories, symbols of spiritual things by which the divine truths can be communicated to man.

Baptism, immersion in or bath of water, was administered to infants in accordance with the apostolic tradition. It symbolized the soul's purification or cleansing from all stain of sin and malice. Thus, it was considered a rebirth, all former sins are erased through divine grace (Comm. John VI. 17). The rite of unction or confirmation appears to have been a part of the baptismal rite (Comm. Rom. V. 8ff.)

Origen speaks often of the Eucharist or Holy Communion. He believed it to be one of the most important mysteries of the Church. It was considered a thanksgiving and prayer to God and a source of sanctification for those who partook of the sacrament in the proper frame of mind (Celsus VIII. 33, 57). The kiss of peace accompanied the sacrament of the Eucharist and was also given after prayers (Hom. Romans X. 33; Comm. Canticles I.).

Prayer was an important rite of the Church. It was man's means of communicating with God, which enabled man to enter into a union with the divine spirit and to share in the divine life. Prayer, according to Origen, was a source of divine grace and had a purifying effect on an individuals existence. It was to be offered at least three times a day, facing the east, either standing or kneeling with outstretched hands and up-lifted eyes (On Prayer 12, 31; Hom. Num. V. 1). Prayers, in general, were conducted in the popular language of each country (Cels. VIII. 37).

In addition to the religious observances, the two Testaments, Old and New, were of major significance. They were considered the Church's absolute, authoritative body of writing, the decisive criterion of dogma; the source from which the Church derived its catechetical material.

IV. The Christian Community

Ideally, Origen considered the Christian community as a group of individuals who following reason have been able to detach themselves from all material things and to live in agreement with God's laws. The Church was composed of a harmonious body of believers animated by Christ, and consisted of a hierarchy in which every Christian had a place according to his degree of spiritual development. Compared with the secular community of a city, to which Origen compares the Christian community, it is a virtuous, dependable and tractable group, governed in the main by individuals of superior moral character and worthy of their position. The secular assembly, on the other hand, is riotous and its senators and governors given to intrigue (Cels. VI. 48; IV. 26; III. 30).

In reality, however, the Christian community during Origen's time was quite different from the idealized picture that he presents in his apologetic work, *Against Celsus*. The community appears to have been large and diversified, of varying educational and social backgrounds. Many of the old Christian families of wealth, political and social position were unaccepting of the new converts, particularly those of lesser social standing (Comm. Matt. XV. 26). In his writings, especially the commentaries and the homilies, Origen often reproaches and criticizes the Christians for their lack of faith and neglect of religion. Although there still remained traces of the miraculous occurrences and charismata found in the early church, faith and interest in religion, except in a superficial way, were on the decline. The Christians attended church infrequently, were disinterested in the study and understanding of the Scriptures and, in general, their actions and way of life were submerged in vice and immorality (Hom. Gen. X. 1, 3; Hom. Ezech. VIII. 2ff.; Hom. Jos. X. 1). Some Christians had a superior attitude about their Christian ancestry (Comm. Matt. XV. 26). Others were proud because of their wealth or position (Hom. Jer. XII. 8). Comparing the Christians of his time with those of earlier years, Origen complains that there are few who could be considered true believers. (Hom. Jer. IV. 3).

Origen also sharply reprimands the clergy for their ambition which caused them to accept favors and to intrigue for higher offices and rank (Hom. Num. XXII. 4; Comm. Matt. XVI. 22), for their pride which was worse than that of tyrants, and for their use of nepotism to fill high ecclesiastical positions (Comm. Matt. XVI. 8). Some clergy, it appears, were doing little more than performing the liturgical functions. They would not even rebuke the evils of society, lest they should fall out of favor with the people (Hom. Josh. VII. 6). The Church during the latter part of the third century was suffering the popular evils of a large, cosmopolitan, powerful diverse society.

V. Religious and Philosophical Background

The first centuries of the Christian era were a time of great transition and unrest. It was a period in which the values by which the ancient world had lived were steadily being uprooted. By the middle of the second century of the present era, the Roman Empire was witnessing a sucession of barbarian invasions, bloody civil wars, various recurring plagues, famines and economic crises. Moreover, the cosmopolitanism of the Empire, the fusion of races, customs, cultures and religions was gradually destroying the State religion, which had served as the basis of the political, social and intellectual life. This period, which began in the early part of the second century and continued throughout the third century, was one of general material and moral insecurity. The unsettling conditions of the period led men to long and search for "soteria"—salvation—a release from the burdens of finitude, the misery and failure of human life. During this period, there was an increase in

9

mystery religions and cults that have their origins in Syria, Persia, Egypt, Babylonia and Asia Minor. The old mysteries of Samothrace and Eleusis as well as others enjoyed renewed and increased popularity. These cults and religions with their purification rites, their enthusiasm and ecstasy and their rewards of immortality through deification, offered a solution to the spiritual needs of the populace. Philosophy also was attempting to find the answer to the religious problems of the people. The skepticism of Epicureanism and the austere ideals of Stoicism, which had a great influence on the lives of the intellectuals for more than four centuries, were no longer adequate to satisfy the religious longings of the people during this time. The result was a return to Platonism. The thinkers of the time believed that they found in the teaching of Plato a philosophy which satisfied their religious needs. This new form of Platonism, which had absorbed many of the ideas of Aristotle, the Stoics and the Neo-Pythagoreans, influenced the thought of the various philosophical and religious movements since the beginning of the Christian era. Ideas derived from this eclectic Platonism are found in the works of the first century Philo of Alexandria, a key representative of Jewish Hellenistic thought.

By the latter part of the second century, the Platonic revival had produced a philosophical movement, Middle Platonism, which gained great prominence. The chief objective of the movement was to solve the problem of man's destiny and salvation through a philosophical system of the universe. Although fundamentally inspired by the teachings of Plato, Middle Platonism also combined elements of Aristotelian logic, Stoic psychology and ethics and Pythagorean mysticism in varying degrees by different philosophers of the time. However, despite its loosely knit and highly diversified character, there exists some degree of uniformity in Middle Platonic speculation, which makes some general remarks about it possible. Their most significant contribution to the history of philosophy and theology was to bring together and equate the supreme Divine Mind of Aristotle and the Platonic world of Forms and Ideas.

Middle Platonism postulates a hierarchy of three divine primary beings, at the head of which is the Divine Mind or God—the first principle of reality. The supreme God is often called the One or the Good and is a simple, changeless and transcendent being, having no direct contact with the material world and inaccessible to the human mind in this life, except in rare and brief flashes of illumination. In the supreme Mind, the Middle Platonists placed the Platonic ideas, the eternal forms which, according to Plato, constitute the archetypal models of all existing things in the universe. These forms or patterns exist eternally in the mind of the first God and are the models upon which the cosmos is created. Being unchanging and transcendent, the Supreme God does not create. He derives from himself a second Mind or God, subordinate to and dependent on the first God, who creates and governs the world. The third principle in the Middle Platonic hierarchy is the World Soul. According to the Middle Platonists, human souls are parts of the Divine, who have descended into the material world and have become embodied. Thus, the object of man's life is to free himself from the world of matter and return to his place in the Divine. This conception of man's life and destiny had a significant influence on later philosophic thought, pagan and Christian. Middle Platonism provided the environment in which Origen's mind was trained and in which his ideas were formed.

VI. Origen's Thought and Method

Origen was a voluminous writer. However, only about a third of his writings are extant today. His works may be divided into five main areas. These include (1) exegetical works, writings on the text of the Old and New Testament found in three different literary forms—(a) scholia or brief notes on various difficult passages of the Scriptures, (b) homilies, usually addressed to popular audiences, and (c) commentaries or lengthy expositions; (2) critical works, the Hexapla or six-column Bible, a textual criticism of all the available texts of the Old Testament, both Greek and Hebrew; (3) apologetical works in defense of Christianity against paganism; (4) dogmatic works which state Origen's views on various questions and issues of Christian dogma; and (5) practical works on prayer, on martyrdom and on Easter, as well as letters to individuals.

His writings are of a diverse and complex nature. For example, his homilies in general reveal a humble and devout Christian, whereas his commentaries, especially those on St. Matthew and St. John and his dogmatic and apologetic work, *First Principles* and *Against Celsus* respectively indicate a very sophisticated student of philosophy, well-versed in the Platonic tradition of his day. The complex nature of his work has perplexed many scholars and present day interpreters of his writings. It has led some of his interpreters to stress the biblical nature of his writings and to consider him a biblical scholar and Christian mystic, while others have emphasized the speculative character of his work and classify him as a Neoplatonic philosopher.[4] However, Origen connot be understood as "either-or." He was not only a student of philosophy, but also a Christian theologian. In fact, he was first and foremost a student and teacher of theology. The Bible was to him the only means by which man could receive the divine truths. It is through the understanding of Scripture that an individual can find the way to knowledge of God and to regain his original pure state and likeness to God. His intense interest in and knowledge of philosophy led him to attempt to explain his understanding of the Christian beliefs in the philosophical terms of his day. However, although Origen makes use of several concepts and terminology found in contemporary philosophical thought, many of his views are a result of Biblical scholarship developed by means of allegorical exegesis of the Scriptures. The fundamental aim of Origen's expository writings is set forth in the preface of his work *First Principles*. In it he states that the Holy Apostles, in their teachings, set forth only the basic doctrine of the Christian faith, without their making any attempt to investigate or explain the reasons or bases of these doctrines. They left these questions for discussion by future theologians (pref. 3). It was Origen's determination to provide such discussion. From these discussions, he also hoped to demonstrate the important functions of Christianity as the new paideia—the educative force of all mankind. He employed the contemporary philosophical concepts to express his Christian thought in an intelligible manner, and adopted the views that could be used to serve as possible means for the explication of the Christian account of God, the world and man, his nature and destiny. These concepts he recast into a Christian mold to agree with his understanding of the Church's teachings. Thus, a true picture of Origen is revealed when his works are treated as a whole, when his Scriptural exegeses and his speculative theories are treated and interpreted together; when he is considered both a biblical theologian and a philosopher.

Knowledge of Origen's thought is not complete. A large portion of his works has been lost. Furthermore, although many of his important treatises survive, they have been preserved not in the Greek text, but in fourth-century Latin translations. Much of the translation is inaccurate, making some parts difficult to interpret. This is true of several of the commentaries, homilies and especially of the *First Principles*, which contains some of Origen's most speculative theories. Of the Greek fragments of the various homilies and commentaries which have survived, the authenticity of several has been questioned and others have been proven to be summaries of the original material. Therefore, it is not absolutely certain that what they relate is Origen's true thought. On the other hand, the text of his great apologetic work, the *Against Celsus*, survives in its entirety and in Greek.[5]

2

First Principles: BKS. I–III[1]

I. Introduction

One of the main works of Origen's early period is his *First Principles* (*De Principiis*). It was written in Alexandria between A.D. 220 and 230. Most scholars agree that it was written no later than A.D. 225. Unfortunately, the work is not preserved in the original Greek but in a Latin translation. It was translated at the end of the fourth century by Rufinus of Aquileia who altered many of Origen's views in order to bring his thoughts on certain points into conformity with the Church's views at the time. All that is preserved of the Greek text are several fragments in the *Philocalia*, a collection of extracts from Origen's works compiled by Basil and Gregory Nazianzus, and in the letter of the Emperor Justinian I. In the main, the fragments consist of Book III, Chapter I, and Book IV, Chapter I–III of the text.

First Principles is Origen's attempt to provide a coherent, broad interpretation of Christian doctrine in defense of orthodox Christianity against the Gnostic heresies. However, it is not a systematic, fully developed, orderly system of Christian doctrines and dogmas as found in later theological works. Most of his views are exploratory rather than dogmatic. They are possible answers or personal opinions about various Christian beliefs that were not answered by dogma or tradition. Frequently, he presents alternatives and leaves the reader to determine the correct view. At other times, Origen recommends views to the Church to be judged and evaluated. On several important issues, the Church judged his recommendations very critically and rejected them. Nonetheless, despite the Church's harsh evaluation of the *First Principles*, the text had a very influential effect on the future development of Christian thought.

Thus, Origen's starting point is the Christian tradition as it was transmitted by the Apostles. As mentioned above, his aim in the *First Principles*, as well as in his other expository writings, is to inquire, suggest, investigate and/or explain the reasons for or bases of the doctrines set forth but not investigated by the Holy Apostles (pref. 3). In his search for possible answers to many of the questions under discussion, Origen relied heavily on Greek philosophy. He adopted the popular Greek philosophical ideas of his time which could serve as possible tools to explain the Christian faith. These ideas he reshaped, revised and modified in accordance with his understanding of the Christian beliefs.

The work *First Principles* consists of four books. In general, the first book examines the nature of God, the generation, nature and hierarchy of the divine Trinity and its relations towards the created beings. It also discusses the origin, essence and fall of the created beings. The second book deals primarily with the creation and present condition of the material world or cosmos, and man as a fallen, embodied spirit. In the third book Origen concerns himself mainly with the question of the freedom of the individual will and responsibility. The fourth book briefly summarizes the fundamental doctrines discussed in the first three books and discusses the Holy Scriptures, their purpose and threefold meaning.

II. God and Creation

Origen's thought in the *First Principles* begins with the idea of the supreme reality—God—and concludes with the concept of union with Him. Following the Platonic tradition, Origen claims that God is immaterial and should not be thought to be any kind of body, nor to exist in a body (I. 1:6). He strongly argues against the Stoic doctrine of God as a fiery material substance, and against the Epicurean theory of the gods, who are composed of lifeless atoms, and thus subject to change and dissolution (I. 1:1ff). Using the popular Platonic terms of his time, Origen describes God as a simple and indivisible intellectual nature, permitting no addition of any kind. There is in Him no greater or smaller, no higher or lower. He is wholly one, the Monad, the Unit, Mind, the source from which all intellectual nature or mind takes its beginning. As pure Mind, God is incorporeal and eternal. Origen gives proof for the immateriality and eternality of God by arguing from the immateriality of mind.

Origen asserts that mind functions independently of space and bodily magnitude. It neither requires space in which to move and operate, nor is affected by it, as is bodily nature. The nourishment of the mind does not come through intellectual activity and knowledge which are incorporeal. Moreover, the growth of the mind is not in a physical sense, but in an intellectual one. Its growth does not follow the same pattern as the body. Even when a body reaches the state of full growth, the mind can continue to grow through mental activity. In particular, mind is capable of perceiving, understanding and retaining the incorporeal and eternal intellectual truths, a feat which a bodily or material nature is not able to achieve. Thus, mind must be superior to any bodily nature; it must be incorporeal and eternal (I. 1:6–7; IV. 4:9–10). Origen concludes that if mind is free from the limitations of the physical world, is incorporeal and eternal, then God, who is the source of all intellectual existence or mind, is also incorporeal and eternal (*Ibid.*). Being incorporeal, God is also immutable and impassible.

God is also incomprehensible, for He is greater than anything man can know or that can be measured. Although transcendent and incomprehensible, He may be known through the beauty of His works, and He makes His presence known to all. All are aware of His providence, and He reveals

Himself to those who are worthy, the pure in heart, in accordance with their ability to perceive Him (I. 1:5ff). Despite Origen's abstractions in determining God's essence, God is not for him an impersonal and inactive absolute principle. For Origen, God is a personal and active being, intelligent, possessed of self-consciousness and will. Thus God is not Absolute, but Perfect, the perfect being, perfect in all things. As a transcendent, simple and complete unity, God could not directly create a multiple and complex universe. An intermediary is needed, a being who is one yet shares in the multiplicity and complexity of the created beings. This intermediary is the Son or Logos.

According to Origen, the Son or Logos is the first-born of God, the first stage in the transition from the One to the Many. He is the perfect image of God, His wisdom, the reflection of His glory and perfection, the sum-total of His world-ideas. The Logos did not have a beginning in time; He is eternally generated from the essence of the Father. Origen compares the generation of the Logos to an act of the will arising from an inner necessity and proceeding from the mind, without either cutting off any part of the mind or being separated or divided from it. As the direct manifestation of God, the Logos is incorporeal, immutable and perfect. Proceeding from the essence of the Father's power, there was never a time when the Logos did not exist. Origen states that there exists no reason or possibility to think that God ever existed without His wisdom and power, or to assume that there was a beginning of His begetting (I. 2:2–9).

As the image of God's power, the first stage from the simplicity of the One to the manifold, the Logos is less than the Father. He is often described as a "second God"; He is everything that the Father is but on a different or lower level (I. 2:12ff). Similar to the contemporary Greek philosophers, Origen assumes the fundamental principle that the product is always inferior to the producer . While inferior to the Father, the Logos is superior to all other beings, even the highest. He is above everything, above all powers and dominions, every-

18

thing that is known not only in this world but in the world to come. The Logos alone knows God in His entirety, and executes the Father's wish in every detail. He is the intermediary both between God and the created world, and between the world and God. On the one hand, the Logos serves as God's agent in creation and revelation; He is the archetypal source of all rational beings and the creator, governing principle and vital energy of the world. At the same time, He is also the only means by which the created beings can attain knowledge of and union with God (I. 2:6–13). Thus, the Logos is the ultimate power through which the two movements, from the One to the multiple and the return to the One, are eternally reconciled.

The first creation of the Father through the Son or Logos is the Holy Spirit, the third stage in the procession of the godhead. Whereas the ideas of God and of the Logos are similar to the current Platonic cosmological view, the idea of the Holy Spirit can only be known from the Scriptures (I. 3:1). In discussing God and the Logos, Origen speaks both as a philosopher and as a Christian. However, with regard to the Holy Spirit, he speaks primarily as a Christian. Origen states that the Holy Spirit is eternal and incorporeal, but the means by which it came into existence is not exactly known. All that is known about the Holy Spirit by the Church is that It is equal in honor and dignity to the Father and the Son. According to Origen, the Holy Spirit proceeds from the Son and is related to Him as the Son is related to the Father, i.e., It is inferior to Him. Origen arranged the persons of the Divine Triad in descending order. According to him, God, the Logos and the Holy Spirit form an eternal, divine triad, distinct and superior to the created world (Pref. 4; I. 3:5–8).

God's first creation was the intelligible world. This world consisted of a community of a definite number of rational beings, pure intelligences or minds, which Origen calls logika (II. 8:3; 9:1). Although Origen speaks of the logika as being created, they were not created in time. Creation with respect to them means that they had a beginning, but not a temporal one.

They were created from all eternity, but their beginning is difficult to conceptualize. It cannot be distinguished by periods of time, but is of the type that can only be contemplated and perceived by pure intellect and reason (I. 2:2). Origen claims that it is absurd to think that there was ever a time when God's power, wisdom and goodness were inactive. Therefore, he maintains that there must always have been beings upon which God exercised His beneficence and governance. Thus, the pure minds or logika existed from all eternity They existed as the thoughts of God, the eternal forms or ideas in the Mind or Wisdom of God, which is the Logos. Origen maintains that since God's Wisdom has always existed, then there always existed in God's Wisdom the form and outline of all created beings, which were then actualized by the Logos as agent (I. 4:3–5).

Existing within the Logos and created by Him through an effluence of God's goodness and love, the pure intelligences or minds were incorporeal, immortal and perfect, participating in the life of the Logos and in perfect communion with God. Since there is neither diversity, change or lack of power in God, He created all beings equal and alike. As created beings, the pure minds are necessarily subject to change and movement; they do not inherently possess goodness in their being; it is given to them by God. Therefore, the power and freedom of movement and change was granted to them in order that the goodness which they possess through God's beneficence might become their own, by being preserved through their own free will. However, the rational minds or beings grew weary of continuously contemplating God. Being lazy, they tended to neglect the good because it required too much effort. Their neglect of the good gave rise to its withdrawal, for what is granted may be taken away. This happens when the soul turns away from, or neglects, its goal—the good. To withdraw from the good means to become immersed in evil. Thus rational beings fall into evil to the degree to which they withdraw from the good (II. 9:1–6: IV. 4:9). Like the other contemporary Platonists, Origen upheld the Socratic-Platonic principle that a rational being would not deliberately and knowingly select evil. Therefore, he explains the fall of the rational beings as a result of their inherent changeability, their laziness or weariness which caused them to make the wrong choice, to neglect God and thus to fall into evil. As a result, the fall of the rational beings was not a deliberate act caused simply by their complete freedom of choice. Freedom is for Origen the ability of the created spirit to change, to develop and to grow by advancing toward God or to neglect the good, and become abased.

Having fallen away from God's love, the rational beings were estranged from Him and became "souls"—"psyche"—a term which Origen derived from "psychesthai", to grow cool (II. 8:3). A similar explanation for the term "psyche" is found in Plato[2] and mentioned by Aristotle.[3] It was also adopted by the Stoics who believed that the soul springs from the cold air surrounding us, and that it first enters the body at the moment that the newborn child gasps its first breath.[4] The soul's estrangement from God caused them to lose their initial unity and equality and to take on various types of forms and material textures. The material and form of a soul's body was determined by the degree of its estrangement from God.

Although the body was created for the rational beings after their fall away from God, no rational being can ever exist without a body (II. 2:1–2: IV. 3:15). Materiality is necessary to the existence of all created natures, and thus provides a distinct differentiation between the created and the uncreated—the Trinity. Although Origen sometimes speaks of rational beings as incorporeal (I. 7:1 ff.), he does not mean that they are immaterial in the same sense as the Trinity. Incorporeality with regard to the created beings means a body of a fine, ethereal and invisible nature, consisting of a pure texture that it can only be conceived by God (I. 6:4 IV. 3:15). According to Origen, matter in itself is without form or qualities. It is a common changeable substratum which is capable of receiving the forms of every type of body and capable of assuming the most diverse transformations. Gross material elements may be refined into a finer or more subtle state, while fine ethereal bodies may become coarse and heavy. The texture and form of a body depends on the will and moral development of the individual being. The more an individual soul advances towards God, the finer the shape and texture of the body in which it is enveloped. On the other hand, the more a soul's will is opposed to God's, the coarser its material and the more unattractive its bodily form (II. 1:4, 2:2). Thus, as the rational beings' love of God continued to "cool" and they fell further away from Him, the form and texture of their bodies also changed in proportion to the degree of each one's estrangement from the Creator (I. 4:1)

III. The Cosmos

The cosmos, or material universe was created after the primal fall to provide a penitential dwelling for the rational beings that have lapsed from God. According to Origen, all the rational creatures neglected God to varying degrees, with the exception of the soul of Christ. However, God made the creatures for a purpose, that they might willfully and voluntarily enjoy perfect communion with Him. Therefore, He provided the discipline and means through which they should attain this end. He created bodies for them which express their character and serve as a medium for their training. The beings who fell only a short distance from God retained their ethereal nature, but in a somewhat coarser state. They became the stars, planets and the angels in their various degrees of hierarchy. Those creatures that fell a greater distance from God were embodied in an earthly human frame. The rational beings who turned completely against God became demonic or evil spirits, and are clothed in dark, coarse and unattractive but invisible bodies (I. 8:1–3; II. 2:1, 6:5, 9:2–3). Simultaneously with the bodies of the fallen beings, God created the material universe to serve as a place for educating and disciplining the souls, a place through which and from which the souls must rise to apprehend and become once again a part of the world of ultimate reality (III. 5:4–5).

Thus, according to Origen, the sensible universe is not as the Gnostics believed an accidental result of fallen spirits, but was created by God through His goodness and love as a penitential dwelling for fallen beings. Although a symptom of evil, the material universe is not in itself evil. It is a grand and beautiful creation, an image of the intelligible universe, God's second-best creation. It manifests God's goodness and love for the created beings, a means of restoring them to their original pure state (II. 1:2). As with the intelligible universe, the material universe was created by God, by means of the Logos, out of nothing—absolute non-being (III. 5:4). However, unlike the intelligible universe, the sensible world is not eternal. It was created in time and will end in time (I. 6:2, 8:4). Within the material universe is a hierarchy of rational beings. This hierarchy, which begins with the archangels and descends downward through the various levels of angels and other heavenly beings, to the various conditions among men and finally to the demonic powers—the lowest level of being, is not due to God's original intention for the rational beings. That is, the rational beings were not originally created by God as manifesting the diversity existing within the created order. It was due to the differences among the souls in the degree of their fall. The diversities are infinite in number, in order to allow for the different types of training and discipline necessary for every kind of nature (II. 9:2–6).

Although of diverse parts and of many functions, the world is not of internal discord, but is maintained in perfect order and balanced equilibrium by God's Providence through the Logos. The Logos governs and keeps in order the entire universe as a huge monstrous animal is held together by one soul, preventing the world from disintegration by guiding each soul within the world back to its proper place in the Divine (II. 1:2–3). According to Origen, the Logos is the instrumental cause of the world's existence and the divine force from which all life is derived and sustained. It is the Logos who organizes the cosmos and envelops and supports it as the soul does the body. Moreover, the Logos takes a personal interest in each soul. He guides and helps each one individually to return to its source, in accordance with each soul's need of Him and its ability to receive Him.

As a training school for souls, the sensible world is not the most comfortable place of existence for the soul, nor is it intended to be. While in the material cosmos, man is subject to all types of punishments, evils and afflictions. He is continuously struggling against the principalities and powers of wickedness and evil (III. 2:1–2). However, these misfortunes should not be counted against God's goodness, for they contribute to the training and pedagogy of the soul. Everything that happens in the world happens in accordance with God's divine plan and purpose. This does not mean that God wills all occurrences. God does not will evil or sinful acts, He wills only what is good. However, God often does not prevent evil acts from occurring. He permits them to happen and employs them as educational measures either for an individual, a group of individuals or for the whole universe (III. 2:6–7).[5]

IV. Man and His Relation to God

Origen does not present a precise, clearly defined doctrine of man. His view of man's nature is vague and inconsistent. The reason for this appears to be that man's nature is not clearly stated in the Scriptures and teachings of the Church (Pref. 5). Therefore, Origen merely presents and discusses the two views found in and substantiated by the Scriptures, (1) that man possesses two souls, a rational and an irrational and (2) that man possesses one soul, a part of which is rational and a part irrational. The decision as to which view is preferable he leaves to the reader (III. 4:5).

Origen states that man is of a threefold nature. He consists of a rational spirit, soul and body. In accordance with the Scriptures, he sometimes speaks of man's rational part as spirit or rational soul. At other times, he speaks of one soul in man and distinguishes two parts within it, a rational and an irrational part, which correspond respectively to man's spirit and soul (II.

24

8:1–5; III. 4:1; IV. 2:1) The spirit or rational part of man descends or is implanted from heaven and joins with the earthly body by means of an irrational or earthly soul, and this constitutes the being "man". The earthly soul is produced along with the earthly body and it cannot subsist apart from it (III. 4:1–2). The ambiguity concerning the nature of the human soul is not peculiar to Origen. Similiar statements concerning the soul's parts are found in the thought of other contemporary Platonists of the time, such as the Neoplatonist Plotinus. The division of the soul into "parts" or levels is a means of explaining the soul's amphibiousness; its affinity and association both in the world of intellect and the world of sense. It is an attempt to explain how and to what degree the soul, as an intellectual substance and a member of the intelligible world, participates in the concerns of matter and the material universe.

Concerning man's rational part or mind, Origen claims that it is created by the Logos of God, in the image of God, and shares or partakes of the divine essence (IV. 4:9–10). As a rational spirit, even though it has been estranged from God and has become a soul, nevertheless, it always retains within it a spark of the Divine, a germ of goodness (III. 4:2; IV. 4:9–10). Participating in the essence of God, man's rational spirit cannot fall into sin completely, a part of it must remain intact. As an image of God, the rational soul of man is immortal, incorruptible and incorporeal. Origen considers it impious to say that man's rational soul or mind, which is capable of perceiving and understanding God and is capable by its own efforts of imitating God and attaining likeness of Him, can ever cease to exist (IV. 4:9–10). Further proof of the soul's immortality and incorruptibility can be shown by the fact that the soul is distinct from the earthly body and separable from it. The soul not only survives the earthly body, but by the power of God also remembers its former existence, another proof of its immortality (II.3:2, 10:4). As a created being, the soul possesses all its attributes through God's power or will. Therefore, as Wolfson points out, the soul's immortality is not by its own nature, but by God's will. The soul, having been created by God and sharing in His nature, will not be destroyed by Him, but God could destroy the soul if He so willed.[6]

As an image of the Divine Mind, man's rational soul or mind is incorporeal. Origen argues against the Stoic doctrine that conceives of soul as a fiery material substance or "pneuma", and against the Epicurean theory of the soul as a compound of lifeless atoms (I. 1ff.). According to Origen, soul or mind cannot be a bodily or material nature, because body is in a continual state of flux and transformation and subject to dissolution. Also, body is inanimate, having no life of its own nor capable of producing life (III. 4:2). Soul, on the other hand, is the principle of life and the organizing force of the body. Thus, soul must be non-material and imperishable. Moreover, in its functions, soul or mind is independent of time, space and bodily aptitude, which affect and control bodily nature. Origen uses the same arguments to prove the incorporeality of man's soul that he uses to prove the immateriality of God. In particular, he stresses that the mind is capable of discerning and understanding the incorporeal, eternal, divine truths, a task impossible for a bodily or material nature. Thus, the rational soul must be superior to any material nature (I. 1:6–7).

Although Origen argues that the soul is in its own nature incorporeal, he claims that it cannot exist without a body. According to him, since the fall of the logika or rational beings, no being, with the exception of the Holy Trinity has ever existed, nor can exist apart from a bodily relationship (II. 2:1–2; IV. 3:15). Adopting the popular Platonic theory at the time of the celestial or ethereal body which envelops all souls,[7] Origen states that the rational beings, when they first lapsed from God, were enveloped in a body of a fine, ethereal and invisible nature (I. 4:1, 8:1ff.). As a soul fell further away from God, the nature of its body changed. It changed from a fine, ethereal and invisible body to a body of a coarser and more solid state, in proportion to the degree of its fall. However, as an individual soul purifies itself and turns back to God, the nature of its body is transformed into a purer and more subtle state. The heavenly

26

body is sometimes referred to as incorporeal, because of its heavenly purity and clarity and because it is perceptible only to the mind. The purity and subtleness of the body with which a soul is enveloped depends on the moral development and perfection of the soul to which it is joined (I. 6:4; II. 2:2; IV. 3:15). Origen claims that there are varying degrees of purity and subtleness even among the celestial and spiritual bodies (II. 10:2).

The body that is permanently attached to the soul is, like the soul, eternal. Although the soul's body is capable of being transformed in accordance with the soul's dignity and perfection, it can never be destroyed nor discarded by the soul (I. 6:4; II. 2:2; IV. 3:15). Within the soul's ethereal body, Origen places the form or "eidos" of the individual body. This form is distinctive in each individual and remains eternally unchanged (II. 10:3). The concept of the ethereal body is of great importance to Origen's view of the resurrected body. By maintaining its perpetuity, and placing within it the distinctive form of each individual body, Origen is able to preserve the individual identity of each earthly body with its resurrected spiritual body.[8]

Following the popular Platonic concept, Origen states that the soul stands midway between the body and the mind, and fluctuates between the two. The term "soul" in this context refers to man's discursive or reasoning faculty, the part of man which constitutes his distinct and particular individuality. Man's reasoning faculty is of an indifferent character, receptive to either vice or virtue. Thus, it can unite either with the spirit-mind, or with the body, or it can remain midway between the two (II. 8:4; III. 4:2–4). Man's struggle consists of the attempt of the mind and the body to gain control of the soul. The choice that the soul makes determines man's actions and individuality. If the mind attains mastery, man achieves likeness to God; if the body wins, man is plunged into evil and is controlled by the passions and desires. However, the body in itself is not evil. In its own proper nature it is completely inert, unable to feel or experience anything. Therefore, the passions and emotions belong to the synthesis of body and soul, to the body animated by soul. However, the animated body is not the true cause of evil, but the choice that the soul makes (III. 4:2–4).

In his intermediate position between the angels and the demons, man is subjected to the influence of both the angels and the demons. His moral struggle is made more difficult by the demons and made easier by the angels. Every man has a guardian angel who aids and encourages him to return to his original state of purity, and an evil angel who tries to lure him into evil (III. 2:1–4, 3:4). Similar to many of the writings of his time, the idea of angels and demons as ministers and governors of the various elements in the sensible world dominates Origen's view of the condition of man and the world. Thus, all of life is a struggle among unseen powers, evil powers striving against the good to gain dominance of man. However, man at all times possesses within himself the power or faculty to choose between good and evil. According to Origen, freedom of choice is an eternal attribute of man's rational nature and rests solely with the individual person. Nonetheless, nothing that happens to man is without God's knowledge and providential guidance. However, God's guidance never interferes with man's freedom of choice. God persuades, admonishes, sustains and rewards, but never constrains nor in any way overrules the free will of the individual soul (III. 1:19).

Origen maintains that man's goal in life should be to realize his true nature which is divine, and to strive to regain his original pure state and likeness to God. This, man can acquire through his imitation of the Logos (III. 6:1; IV. 4:9–10). However, the journey back to God is long and difficult, for the soul is continually beset by temptations that try to lure it into sin. In order for the goal to be achieved, man's steady and persistent effort is required, together with God's continuous guidance and help. According to Origen, man does not possess a sufficiently strong will or the ability to obtain union with God through his own insight or self-knowledge, or by merely imitating Christ. At every step of the way, the soul requires the aid of the Logos, who enlightens the soul in accordance with the soul's maturity and spiritual progress (III. 2:2, 5). As the soul advances by successive stages back to God, it is gradually and proportionately endowed with divine grace. It is through the grace of the Logos that the soul is led gradually from a knowledge of self to the battle against sin, to practices of asceticism, to the mystical ascent and finally to union with the Divine. In other words, it is grace that provides the soul first with the moral power with which to struggle against sin; and then with the intellectual insight, the power to perceive and understand fully the work of God, the mystical divine truths which heretofore had been hidden from it.

Origen views the ascent of the soul as a gradual inner, spiritual development of the soul. It is a process by which the soul diligently strives to purify itself, a continual advancement towards the good. First, it purifies itself morally; then, with the grace of God, it develops the sense or knowledge to discern the real from the temporal. As it continues to be illuminated by the Logos, it advances forward until it comes to live purely in the spirit and unites with the Logos.

However, the soul's complete union with God cannot be obtained in this life, while the soul is clothed in a human body. Man's bodily nature is an impediment both to the soul's continuing and uninterrupted vision or contemplation of God and its fitness for union with Him (III. 6:3). While in the earthly body, the soul is too weak and unstable to attain complete union with God, even for a rare and brief instant. The soul's complete and lasting unity with God can be achieved only after death, and for many souls, whose progress is very slow, unity with God may not even be achieved in this age (II. 11:7; III. 6:1–3).

Origen claims tht the process of the soul's education and purification is a long and gradual one, developing stage by stage in the course of infinite and immeasurable ages. The process is realized in each soul gradually and separately. Thus, the education of the soul is an age-long spiritual adventure, beginning in this life and continuing after death (II. 11:6–7; III. 6:6). According to Origen, there is no soul that has been completely purified in this life. Adopting the terminology of the popular doctrines of astral or celestial eschatology found in many of the writings of the second-third centuries, he states that after death the souls of the good go to a remote place of the earth, an earthly paradise which was probably situated somewhere within or beneath the earth (II. 11:6).[9] There they are taught the terrestrial truths and are given insight into the course of future events. In accordance with the individual soul's ability to apprehend these truths, the soul ascends from this lower paradise to the region of the air. There it understands the nature and reason of the ordering of that region. From there it ascends to the sphere of the planets, which Scripture calls heavens. In each sphere, the soul undergoes further purification and discovers the secrets of that region. Finally, after the soul has passed through each successive stage of the heavens and has been purified, with its body increasingly becoming more subtle in texture, it once again becomes a pure spirit. It rises in the pure ether to God and enters into the Kingdom of Heaven. There it contemplates the pure essences "face to face" and can see and comprehend the invisible mysteries (II. 11:6–7). In other words, the individual who has turned to Christ and has devoted his life on earth to the understanding of the divine truths, will enter a state of greater awareness after death. Thus, he will be able to progress more rapidly to a spiritual state. The spheres of the heavens represent the levels or stages of purity through which the soul passes before it arrives at a purely spiritual state (II. 11:3ff.).

The evil souls are unable to make the ascent. They remain beneath the earth in hell, where they undergo punishment by fire. According to Origen, the fires of hell are not material, but they are a state of mind. They are the torments of conscience, the soul's remembering of all its evil deeds. Origen calls the fires of hell the penalty and torture of the soul's want of cohesion; it is the punishment the soul must experience because of its unstable and disordered condition (II. 10:4–7). However, God's judgement is not vindictive, but is used only for the purpose of educating and purifying. Therefore, the pains of hell which are disciplinary in purpose are temporary and not eternal (II. 10:4–6,8).

V. Free Will

The question of the freedom of the individual will is of great importance to Origen and constitutes the ethical basis of his thought. He devotes the major portion of the third book of the *First Principles* as well as the sixth chapter of the treatise *On Prayer* to the problem. Origen attempts to establish the existence and explain the nature of free-will by drawing on numerous passages both from the Old and New Testament. However, as Jackson[10] correctly points out, Origen's doctrine of free will is dependent more upon the Platonic and Stoic theories of freedom than upon Scripture. According to him, Origen combines the Platonic transcendental view of freedom, i.e., that a rational soul is distributed in each epoch of its life in accordance with its exercise of freedom in the preceding epoch, with the Stoic analysis of the internal structure of freedom. He then modifies these views with Scriptural doctrine.[11]

Origen bases his proof of the existence and nature of freedom on the principle of movement and the type of movement. He distinguishes between those movements which arise from within and those that originate from without. Origen claims that some things, such as logs of wood and stones and all things which are held together by the constitution of their material or by their physical structure, are moved solely from without. Things such as animals, plants, fire and springs and others, which are held together by their structure or by soul, are moved from within. Of the latter group there are two types, the non-living who are moved out of themselves and the living or ensouled things—those who possess a soul—who are moved from within themselves. The ensouled beings include the animals and the rational beings. Animals possess the imaginative faculty which produces images or impressions. The images call forth the various impulses, and it is by these impulses that the animal is moved. For example, the image of a web arises in a spider, and the impulse to weave it follows. Similarly, in the bee there is an impulse to produce a honeycomb. However, man possesses, in addition to the imaginative faculty, a reasoning faculty—a logos. This enables him to judge the images which arise and to determine which are worthy to be acted upon and which should be rejected. When man selects the right images he is praised, when he chooses the evil ones he is condemned (III 1:2).[12] It is not within man's power to control the images or impressions which are presented to him. However, man through the use of his reasoning faculty can decide how to use these impressions. To deny that man is capable of judging the uncontrollable external impressions, that he is incapable of being moved from within, is to say that man is not a rational being, that he is not even a living animal (III. 1:3.).[13]

Since man is not controlled by external images and impressions and can accept or reject them as he sees fit, there is no justification for blaming external causes for man's sins (III. 1:4–5). Thus, according to Origen, freedom pertains not only to the rational being's ability to move from one state to another, but also to the use that the rational being makes of the impressions that are presented to it. It is man's responsibility to elevate his reasoning power to a higher level by educating and disciplining it. In this way he will be better able to distinguish among impressions and reject the ones that would lead him to evil (III. 1:4). Man's use of his free-will determines his status in this life and the next.

According to Origen, God has been aiding and attempting to train the souls to make the right choices and to improve their status ever since the original fall. God has never ceased to be concerned with the salvation of man. By means of the Logos, He has been training and educating mankind from the time of creation. To Origen, the whole of history has been influenced by Divine Providence, God's plan for the salvation of mankind.

His thought represents a true philosophy of history. Origen's view of human history encompasses both the facts of biblical history and the history of Greek thought.

VI. The End of All Things

Origen's teachings on the end of all things is unique to his thought. It is summed up in his doctrine of the "apokatastasis", or the restoration of all rational beings to their original state of spiritual purity and equality. The doctrine is determined by the principle that the end should resemble the beginning. In accordance with this principle, Origen claims that at an appointed time known only to God all rational souls, the souls of all man, angels, celestial beings and demons will be purified and will voluntarily return to their original state of perfection (I. 6:1; II. 10:8). However, the individual soul's education and purification is a long and gradual one, developing stage by stage in the course of infinite and immeasureable ages with each soul continually beset by temptation and sin. Moreover, because of the soul's inherent instability, it continually vacillates between good and evil. Thus, the process of purification is realized in each soul gradually and separately at different levels and speeds (III. 6:6). Therefore, it may take more than one aeon before the "apokatastasis" is achieved. Nonetheless, God's infinite love and patience will prevail and will wear down the resistance of even the most rebellious souls. Even Satan himself will of his own free will acknowledge God's excellence and return to Him. God will then be all in all. Each soul will be completely purified and one with God. The purified soul will no longer be conscious of anything besides or other than God, but will think God and see God and hold God and God will be the mode and measure of its every movement and His rule will be universal (II. 11:7; III. 6:2–3).

At the "apokatastasis", men will be reunited with their bodies. Origen believed that the resurrected body will be the same as that which man inhabited on earth, but with a difference. It will be different because it will be spiritual, of a finer, more ethereal quality than the earthly body and suitable to its heavenly environment (I. 8:4; II. 2:2, 10:1, 3; III. 6:4–6). Just as man's soul at the time of the "apokatastasis", or restoration, will have become pure spirit, the body, which will continue to serve the spirit, will be purified and attain a spiritual quality and nature (II. 3:2; III. 6:6).[14]

Once the rational beings have returned to their original state of purity, it is uncertain whether they would remain in that state. Origen claims that the freedom of the will is an eternal attribute of the rational spirits. Thus it is possible that the rational spirits may lapse or fall again. Origen does not take a definite stand on the question of whether the souls, once restored to their original purity, will fall again. In fact, he often avoids giving a definite answer. However, he seems to favor the view that once the souls have united with God their love for Him would be so strong that they could not possibly fall away from God again.[15]

3
First Principles
BK. IV

I. The Purpose of the Scriptures

Although Origen in the development of his ideas employs several concepts and the terminology of the contemporary philosophical thought of his time, his views are primarily the result of Biblical scholarship. The fourth and last book of the *First Principles* is primarily concerned with Origen's views on the Holy Scriptures, both the Old and New Testament. It deals with the questions of the purpose, inspiration and interpretation of the Bible.

According to Origen, the Holy Scriptures are divine, they are the living word of God composed through the Spirit of God (IV. 2:9). They are a reflection of the invisible or divine world. Their contents are the outward forms of certain mysteries and the image of divine truths (Praef. 8; IV. 1:1, 6). As a result, the prime purpose of scripture is not to present a literal meaning or a narrative of historical events. Its purpose is to convey divine and eternal truths. These deeper truths are hidden under the letter of scripture (IV. 3:4ff.). To reveal and correctly expound and interpret the hidden meaning of the Scriptures was of utmost importance to Origen, and he considered it his primary task. He discovered and interpreted the deeper truths or mysteries of scriptures by means of allegorical interpretation, based on the Alexandrian tradition.

Allegorism in the interpretation of the Scriptures had been in use at Alexandria long before the time of Origen. It had been applied to the Old Testament by the Jews and to the New Testament by the Gnostics. Philo systematically applied the method of allegory to derive from the Old Testament both a literal and a spiritual meaning. The Gnostics used allegory to interpret the Gospel of St. John in the interest of Valentinian theology; and Clement of Alexandria practiced and encouraged allegorical exegesis. He regarded it as part of the Church's rule of faith, and attributes both a literal and a spiritual meaning to the Scriptures.[1] Origen continued the Alexandrian tradition of allegorizing the Scriptures, finding the true and deeper meaning of the Scriptures in the philosophical concepts which lie beneath its literal and historical husk. In this manner, he attempted to bring into accord, systematically the philosophy of Christianity with its documents.

Thus, according to Origen, scripture has both an obvious, a literal meaning, and a hidden or allegorical meaning. In fact, Origen claims that all of scripture contains a spiritual or deeper meaning, but every scriptural passage does not have a literal meaning. The reason for this is that the literal meaning often proves to be an impossibility. Where there is both a spiritual and literal or historical meaning, the spiritual is of greater importance than the narrative of historical events (IV. 3:5). The hidden or deeper meaning of scripture is concealed from the majority of readers. It can only be perceived by those on whom the grace of the Holy Spirit has been conferred in speech, wisdom and knowledge (Paef. 8).

Origen did not establish a definite set of rules for the interpretation and exposition of the Scriptures. However, there are certain basic principles that he seems to have followed throughout his scriptural exegesis. According to Origen, the literal word of the Bible contains two meanings; there is the material or "bodily" meaning and the "allegorical" one. The "bodily" meaning refers to the obvious interpretation of the text, the grammatical meaning within the context of the sentence. In some instances, the obvious or literal meaning is the conclusive one. This is true when the text refers to a historical or actual event. For example, the pronouncement on creation,

"In the beginning God created the heavens and the earth," is a true statement (III. 5:1). However, when the Bible speaks of the first three days of creation as actual days, when neither the sun, moon nor stars had been created; or when it speaks of God planting a paradise or walking therein, these are not actual events. The true meaning in these instances is allegorical. The anthropomorphic expressions attributed to God in these passages are figurative expressions which indicate certain mysteries through a semblance of history and not through actual events (IV. 3:1). Thus, in reading the Scriptures, an individual must discern whether a passage is to be understood literally or allegorically by carefully investigating to what extent the literal meaning is true and possible. Origen seems to have adhered to the general rule that anytime a scriptural passage entails something impossible, absurd or unworthy of God, the literal or "bodily" meaning should be disregarded and should be interpreted allegorically (IV. 3:5). The allegorical meaning of scripture is further divided by Origen into the moral and spiritual. Thus, according to Origen, scripture has, in general, three meanings or senses, the literal, the moral and the spiritual.

II. The Threefold Meaning of the Scriptures

Origen finds proof for the three levels of scriptural meaning—the literal, moral and spiritual—in the Old Testament, in Solomon's Proverbs 22:20ff. From this he argues that scriptures' three meanings are analogous to the three parts of man, body, soul and spirit, and to the three levels of an individual's development—the individual soul's spiritual ascent to union with God and to perfection (IV. 2:4). Thus, Origen recognizes not only various levels of scriptural meaning, but also various classes of Christians ranging from the simple to the perfect.

The literal or historical meaning of scripture is comparable to man's body, and is understood by all Christians. It corresponds to man's initial faith, a simple, unquestioning, trustful faith. This is the faith that is evidenced by the multitude of sincere and simple believers (IV. 2:6). This is not to say that the historical sense is not important, but man must strive to understand the deeper meaning of scripture. Origen is quite aware of the danger of allegorizing all historical events and thus reducing them to timeless myth. The second level of scriptural meaning, the moral or soul, pertains to an individual's moral conduct in life and his proper relation to God. It is apprehended by those individuals who, through a steady and persistent effort, have advanced to a spiritual level of self-knowledge and understanding. In this stage of spiritual development, the individual soul has realized its true divine nature as well as its tendency towards unstable passions and emotions. It has realized not only its goal, unity with God, but also the paths that keep it from attaining and retaining its goal, and it recognizes that it must take up the struggle against sin and the passions. The spiritual or mystical sense of scripture, the most important according to Origen, includes all the divine mysteries. This sense is understood only by those individuals who have attained spiritual perfection, i.e., by those who have attained supremacy over the bodily passions. Man, in this stage of development, has detached himself from the worldly things that are the causes of sin. He is now capable of receiving divine illumination and a more complete understanding of the truth of God's revelation. Complete alienation from the world and its deceptions permits an individual to enter the world of true reality and to comprehend the divine truths. In other words, man has received true gnosis or knowledge; he has passed beyond the things of sense to the contemplation of things incorporeal and eternal. On this level, man is able to comprehend clearly the spiritual or mystical sense of the scriptures, which include the mysteries of God's purpose and doctrines through the ages, past, present and future (IV. 2:4ff.).[2]

Thus, Origen strongly maintained that, in accordance with his spiritual development, an individual can find in Scripture, and only in Scripture, the way to knowledge of God and to the soul's ultimate perfection. This does not mean that Origen was opposed to the study of philosophy. He believed that philosophy was a valuable preparation for revealed theology, but not indispensable in order to receive God's truths, nor adequate to lead man to the understanding of the ultimate truth. This can be accomplished only through divine gnosis or wisdom, which is revealed through the Holy Scriptures.

4

Against Celsus

I. Introduction

The *Against Celsus*, or the *Contra Celsum* as it is more commonly known, is Origen's great apologetical work. It is considered to be one of the most important apologies in the history of the early Church during the second and third centuries. Unlike many of Origen's works which are preserved either as fragments or in fourth century Latin translations, the text of the *Against Celsus* survives in its entirety and in Greek. It is one of Origen's latter works, written, according to Eusebius, when he was over sixty years old (Hist. Eccl. VI. 36).

The treatise consists of eight books and is a point by point refutation of the work *True Discourse*, written by the pagan philosopher Celsus against Christianity. Origen's arguments are presented along with the appropriate quotations from Celsus' work. Thus, both sides of the debate are made available. Origen's division of the work is arbitrary and does not refer to a similar division in the *True Discourse* (III. 81; VI. 81; VII. 70). Celsus' *True Discourse* is not extant. However, a great part of it can be reconstructed from Origen's quotations in the *Against Celsus*. From Celsus' statements, it is believed that the work was written sometime between A.D. 177–180 during the reign of Marcus Aurelius (VIII. 68–75).[1] Celsus' main concern is that the Christians had abandoned and corrupted the ancient tradition (I. 14; V. 35.). The purpose of the work was to convince the Christians to turn away from their religion and to return to the worship of the classical gods and the religion of the State. He hoped to accomplish this by skillfully discrediting the

Christian faith item by item, proving it to be a religion of false doctrines, and thus shaming the Christians back to paganism. Celsus feared that the religious and political isolation of the Christians was creating a division among the populace, weakening the Empire and causing a danger to the welfare and security of the State (VIII. 69–75). Celsus knew his subject well. He knew the Christian facts and dogmas, and claimed to have received this knowledge from the Christian writings (II. 74). An analysis of his texts indicates that he had some familiarity with the writings of the Old Testament; he knew the four Gospels, especially the Gospel of Matthew, and the Christian literature of the period (IV. 52; VIII. 15).[2]

Celsus' work does not appear to have had much impact on the community to whom it was addressed. Christian writers of his time never refer to it. It was not until 65 to 70 years after it was written, about A.D. 246–248, that Origen wrote his refutation. The work was reluctantly undertaken at the request of Origen's friend and benefactor, Ambrose (Pref. 1–4). Following closely Celsus' arguments, the treatise deals with three main discussions, the history of Christianity, the general idea and character of Christianity and the relations of Christianity to national life and religion.

The *Against Celsus* is an important source for the history of Christian thought and life. It is a study of second-third century paganism and developing Christianity, and the intellectual struggle between the two.

II. Theology of Celsus

Celsus' theology is based on the contemporary Platonic ideas of God and his relation to the universe and to man. Thus, according to Celsus, there is one supreme transcendent God who is good, beautiful, happy and immutable (IV. 14).[3] He has no movement, attribute or name (VI. 62–64). God is pure intelligence, the reason of all that exists, the totality of ideas (V. 14), comprehended only by the mind through synthesis, analysis and analogy (VII. 42, 44).[4] God created all reasonable immortal beings, the soul of man and all lower deities (IV. 52; V. 6). The material world and everything mortal was created by the lower deities or demons (IV. 52).[5]

The material universe and all the things within it have been created not for any one group, but for the whole. It does not exist for man anymore than for the wildest of irrational animals (IV. 74, 99). Everything is born and perishes for the preservation, completion and perfection of the whole of nature (IV. 99.). God cares for the whole universe, but has no special concern for any one thing within it, including man. Man is but a small entity within the whole of the universe (IV. 73–99). The world revolves in the same circuit from the beginning to the end. According to the determined cycles, the same things always happened, are now happening, and will happen (IV. 67). Evil is inherent in the material world and dwells among mortals. Celsus, following Plato held that evil is a product of matter and cannot be abolished. It is a part of mortal nature and the material world (IV. 65; VIII. 55).[6] Since the quantity of matter is constant and determined, it follows that the origin and quantity of evil is always the same. There is no increase or decrease of evils in the world (IV. 62, 69, 99). Thus, there is no need for special divine intervention; God does not need to interfere for the correction or improvement of the created world (IV. 69).

God's universal providence is generally exercised by the sun, moon and stars, and regionally exercised through the mediation of the demons or lower deities. According to Celsus, they are all manifestations of God, deities who should be worshipped and venerated (V. 6, 25ff; VII. 68–70; VIII. 25). Celsus considers the lower deities as satraps and ministers of God, similar to the provincial governors of an emperor (VIII. 35). They are the gods of the old national religions, Greek and barbarian alike, to whom local cults are offered; the superintending spirits who guard and protect the various parts of the earth (V. 25, 34). According to Celsus, from the beginning of the world, the different parts of the earth were allotted to different deities or overseers. As a result, different practices of worship and veneration were established by each nation in accordance with the wishes of the deities placed in charge of the nation. The religious practices of each nation are right when they are done in a way that pleases the national overseer. Therefore, the regional deities should be honoured and the traditional local customs and laws of worship should be carefully observed. It is impious to abandon or alter the religious customs which have existed in each locality from the beginning, and a threat to the state (V. 25, 34ff).[7] In fact, the more that the local deities are worshipped, the fuller and more perfect becomes the worship of God (VIII. 66). Moreover, it is not important by what name you refer to God. For there is only one God, one supreme power worshipped in different places under many different names (I. 24; V. 41; VIII. 2, 69). Thus, it is a rebellious utterance to say that "no man can serve two masters;" for the more gods that a man worships, the more pleasing it is to the supreme God since they are all his ministers (VIII. 2), and it is one and the same God who is being worshipped (VIII. 69).

III. Celsus' View of Christianity

Consistent with his theology, Celsus strongly objected to the Christian beliefs. He begins his attack on Christianity by stating that the Church was a secret, and thus an illegal body of barbarious origin which should not exist (I. 1ff). Nevertheless, he states, the Christians do well to work and teach in secret: the death penalty hangs over them (I. 3). Although Celsus thinks that the Christians are foolish for running into danger, he admits that he admires an individual who stands by his beliefs to the point of death, and condemns people who hold Christian beliefs but pretend that they do not or deny them (I. 8). However, the Christians believe and accept doctrines without examination. They believe that blind faith will save them. Blindly they accept the claims of Christ that he is the Son of God, a belief that is not based on logic and reasoning, and is worthy of its adherents, individuals who are in the main uneducated (I. 26–27).

Concerning Jesus and the claims about him, Celsus first attacks him in the person of a Jew and then in the person of Celsus himself. According to the Jew, Jesus fabricated his virgin birth. His mother was a poor, Jewish, country woman who earned her living by spinning, was convicted of adultery, was driven out by her carpenter husband and secretly gave birth to Jesus. Because of his extreme poverty, Jesus left Jerusalem and hired himself out as a workman in Egypt. There he developed his magic powers, and because of them returned home to proclaim himself God (I. 28). This is a much more plausible account of Jesus' claim to divine powers than that held by the Christians. Moreover, why would God choose a poor, unknown woman to bear his son (I. 39)? Thus, claims Celsus, the account of the descent of the Spirit in the form of a dove at Jesus' baptism and the narrative of the Chaldean wise-men who visited him at birth are unreliable. There are no credible witnesses to the appearance of the Holy Spirit in the form of a dove, nor to God's voice adopting Jesus as his son. The only knowledge of the account is given by Jesus himself and by John the Baptist who was also punished with Jesus (I. 41). Moreover, if, as the Christians believe, every man who is born according to divine providence is a son of God, what is the difference between Jesus and everyone else (I. 59)? The Chaldeans' visit to the infant Jesus also does not indicate any evidence of his divine sonship. Moved by a strange impulse, they came to worship the infant Jesus as God and informed King Herod of this. He proceeded to slay all the children that had been born at that time for fear that Jesus might replace him as King. To avoid being slain, he was taken to Egypt secretly. This would not have been necessary if he was the son of God. God would have protected him both from Herod and from those who later crucified him. Why, if he was God's son, did he not become King, but go about begging, cowering from fear, and wandering up and down in destitution with a collection of ten or eleven illiterate and infamous companions (I. 58–66)?

The prophesies proclaimed about the son of God in the Old Testament do not necessarily apply to Jesus. They are applicable to thousands of others far more plausibly who lived before him (I. 49–50: II. 28). Even Jesus' words and deeds are not that noteworthy. Granted, he is known to have healed the sick, raised the dead and multiplied a few loaves, but these so-called miracles are not any different or better than those accomplished by the Egyptian trained sorcerers who for a few obols display their miraculous powers in the market-place. Should these wonder-workers also be considered sons of God, or rather wicked men possessed by an evil demon (I. 67–68). Thus, from all indications it appears that Jesus has no more claim to divine sonship than any other individual. In fact, his claims and pretensions show him instead to be impious, a wicked sorcerer, and one hated by God (I. 71).

To the Jews who had converted to Christianity, Celsus, in the person of the same Jew, rebukes them for abandoning the law of their fathers to follow an imposter, one who never fulfilled his promises and was even abandoned and betrayed by his own disciples (II. 1–9). Taking the various statements written about Jesus in the Gospels, Celsus' Jew, as Origen calls him, attempts to show that not only are they not credible but, on the contrary, prove that Jesus was not the Messiah of God but a charlatan and miracle worker no different from those that have existed through the ages. He begins by accusing the disciples of having invented the statement that Jesus foreknew and foretold all that happened to him. The fact that they happened proves the assertion that he predicted them false. What god, demon or sensible man foreknowing the dangers that would befall him would not attempt to avoid them, rather than encounter the exact events which he had foreseen? If he foretold both the individual who betrayed him and the one who denied him, why did they not fear and respect him as God and refrain from these activities? Furthermore, it is inconceivable that those who were aware that Jesus knew their intentions would still have betrayed and denied him. However, if he foretold these events as a god, then their accomplishment was inevitable. Therefore, a god led his disciples with whom he ate and drank astray, conspiring against them and making them traitors and impious men (II. 17–20).

The Christians exalt Jesus' sufferings, claiming that they were undertaken voluntarily. However, claims Celsus' Jew, if these things had been determined for him by his divine father, then, being a god, they could not be too painful nor grievous to him. Yet, he uttered loud wailings and laments and prayed to be delivered from the tortures saying, "O Father, if this cup could pass by me." He could not even endure thirst as patiently as an ordinary man (II. 23–27, 37). He did not react at all like a god in his suffering, and although the Christians claim that he endured these sufferings for the good of mankind, in order to teach them to despise punishment, he was not able to convince anyone, not even his disciples (II. 38–43).

Celsus accuses the Christians of sophistry when they claim that Jesus as the Son of God is the Logos himself. A man who has been disgracefully arrested and crucified cannot be claimed as the absolute pure and holy Logos (II. 30–31). There is no evidence of his divinity nor of a noble lineage, despite the genealogical accounts given about him in the gospels, which claim that he was descended from the first man and the Jewish Kings (II. 32).

Jesus himself did not claim that his so-called miracles were divine; and it is known that other sorcerers have claimed similar wonders. Even his prediction that he would rise from the dead has been claimed by numerous charlatans to convince the populace in order to deceive them. Pythagoras did this in Italy, his slave Zamolxis to the Scythians and Rhampsinitus in Egypt. Moreover, according to the Christians, Jesus' resurrection was witnessed by a hysterical woman and perhaps by some other one of his followers (II. 55).

If Jesus really wanted to prove his divinity, he either should have disappeared immediately from the cross, or when he arose he ought to have appeared to those who had condemned him and insulted him, and to everyone in general. He no longer needed to fear any man after he had died, if as it is claimed, he was a god. Instead, he appeared secretly to one woman and to his disciples. This action is inconsistent. When he was in the body and disbelieved, he preached unrestrained to all men; after arising from the dead, when he could have established a strong faith, he appeared only to a few of his followers. If Jesus wanted to teach mankind to despise death, after his resurrection he ought to have summoned all men openly to the light and taught them his purpose for coming to earth (II. 63–73). Celsus' Jew concludes his argument with the statement that all these objections were derived from the Christian writings, i.e., the Gospels. The Christians then provided their own refutation. Thus, it could be concluded that Jesus was a mere man, and a man of such a character as the truth itself reveals and as reason demonstrates (II. 79).

After concluding the attacks of the Jew on the person of Christ and his reprimanding of the Jews who had converted to Christianity, Celsus continues the objections to Christianity in his own person. He argues that there is no significant difference between Jews and Christians. Both believe in the prophesy of the coming of a divine saviour or Messiah. They only differ as to whether the one prophesied has come or not (III. 1). Christianity, like Judaism, began as a revolutionary system based on legends with no more credibility than those of the Greeks. The Jews, who Celsus believes were Egyptians by race, revolted against the Egyptian community and religious customs under Moses; the followers of Jesus revolted from the Jewish religious ideas (III. 5). The same spirit of revolt still dominates the Christians. When they were few, they were united, but as they increased in number they divided, and continue to divide, into sects and factions. Each desires to have his own party. The only thing that they all still have in common is the name Christians (III. 9–12). The Christian idea of a divine being is no different from that of the Greeks who believed that Dioscuri, Heracles, Asclepius and Dionysus were men who became gods. Yet, because these men were initially human, the Christians do not consider them divine, although they achieved many noble deeds for the good of mankind. Asclepius, in fact, was seen and is still seen by many, both Greeks and barbarians, healing men, doing good deeds and predicting the future. On the other hand, Jesus, after his death was seen only by a few of his followers, and then as a shadow (III. 22, 24). Blinded by faith, the Christians accept the supernatural beliefs about Jesus' resurrection and ascension without question, and pay homage to him as a god though he was born of a mortal and corruptible body (III. 39–41). Other individuals have also been credited with similar feats, yet they are not considered divine. Abaris the Hyperborean was believed to have ascended carried along by an arrow, and Clazomenian whose soul left his body and he wandered about in a bodiless state. However no one thinks that either of them are a god (III. 31–32). The Christians ridicule the Cretans and others who worship Zeus and reverently show his tomb. Nonetheless, they themselves worship someone who rose from the tomb (III. 43). Thus, concludes Celsus, the Christian doctrines are comparable to those of the Egyptians, which the Christians mock. The Egyptians have magnificent shrines and wonderful temples. However, when entered, one sees represented as a deity an animal, a cat, monkey, crocodile, goat or dog. Although they show many profound mysteries and teach that their worship is not directed to ephemeral animals but to eternal, invisible ideas. The Christian accounts of Jesus do not have anything more worthy of attention than the goats and dogs of the Egyptians (III. 17–19).

Continuing his attacks, Celsus states that the religion of the Christians appeals and caters only to the ignorant and sinful. It is not worthy of the wise and educated, in fact, it excludes them. Their sayings claim, "Let no educated, wise or sensible man approach. For these abilities are considered evil. However, anyone ignorant or uneducated should come forth boldly." By acknowledging that such individuals are worthy of their God, they show that they are interested in and are able to attract only the foolish and dishonorable, the slaves, women and small children (III. 44). Misinterpreting the Christian exhortations to those leading sinful lives, Celsus claims that the

Christians' defense for accepting such individuals is that God was sent for sinners. However, he claims, the real reason is that they cannot convert to Christianity anyone really good or righteous (III. 65).

Concerning the Christian teachers, Celsus accuses them of acting like medical frauds who promise to restore the sick to health, but warn them from visiting a skilled physician lest their lack of training becomes apparent. He also likens them to men suffering from ophthalmia, or eye inflammation, who, in the presence of individuals suffering from the same affliction, accuse those with good eyesight of having defected vision. (III. 75, 79). These men, asserts Celsus, offend and insult God lead wicked men astray with vain hopes by persuading them to avoid anything that is superior on the basis that avoidance of such things will be better for them (III. 78).

One of Celsus' major objections to Christianity was that it has no basis—no authority for its doctrines which are misunderstandings and corruptions of the ancient traditions (III. 16; V. 65) This fact greatly distressed him and he devotes considerable discussion in his treatise to it. As a Platonic philosopher, Celsus strongly stresses the superiority of the philosophy and worship of the Greeks. He approves of the ethical teaching of the Christians, but claims that it is neither new or impressive; it is common to all philosophers (I. 4).

Quoting Plato and other philosophers, Celsus attempts to prove that the Christian doctrines either have been better expressed by the Greeks, or have been corrupted by the Christians.[8] This is true of the Christian understanding of God that is borrowed from Plato. However, it is better expressed by him and without any arrogant claim that it had been announced by God or a Son of God. Nor does Plato claim special knowledge of the divine, but presents the source of his doctrines. Moreover, Plato does not demand blind faith, nor does he suppress any inquiries about his teachings as the Christians do, but seeks to enlighten all individuals by questions and answers (VI. 1, 3, 6–10).[9] Even their view of God as a spirit is not original. It is a borrowing from the Stoics who claim that God is spirit that has permeated all things and contains all things within itself (VI. 71). Their view of God as a supercelestial spirit is respectively a Stoic borrowing and a misunderstanding of a saying from Plato's *Phaedrus*. Plato states that the ultimate being, colorless, formless, incomprehensible, visible only to the mind that is the guide of the soul, lives in the region above the heavens (VI. 19).[10] Moreover, the celestial eschatology of the Christians, the doctrine of the soul's ascent through the planetary spheres after death, is taken from the Persian Mithraic mysteries (VI. 21 ff); and the blessed resting place of the purified souls, which the Christians call heaven, is merely the Islands of the Blest or the Elysian Fields[11] found in the ancient writers (VI. 20; VII. 28). Compared to those of the Persians and Greeks, the Christian eschatological concepts and views of heaven are absurd, fit only for the ears of fools and slaves (VI. 23 ff). In addition, they have misunderstood Plato's doctrine of metempsychosis, or the transmigration of the soul, and teach the resurrection of the body. For the Christians believe that this is the only way that they shall see and know God. They expect to see God with the bodily eye, hear his voice with human ears and touch him with sensible hands (VII. 32–35).

The much discussed Christian humility is a misunderstanding of a saying of Plato which states that, "God having the beginning, end and middle of all that exists, moves on a straight course and in accordance with his nature. Along with God goes justice as the avenger of all transgressions of the divine law. Those who would be happy follow the law orderly and humbly"[12] However, by humble, Plato does not mean, as the Christians, that an individual should humble himself in a disgraceful and undignified manner, kneeling or prostrating himself on the ground, dressing as a beggar and throwing ashes on his head (IV. 15).[13]

The Christian account of the Kingdom of God and Jesus' judgement against the rich which states that, "It is easier for a camel to go through the eye of a needle than for a rich man to enter into the Kingdom of God",[14] have been borrowed from Plato. Jesus' saying is a corruption of the Platonic saying that, "It is impossible for an exceptionally good man to be also exceptionally rich (VI. 16–18).[15] Other misinterpretations or corruptions of the ancient traditions include the Christian view of Satan, and the concept of the Son of God.

Celsus claims that the Christian notion of and belief in Satan springs from a misinterpretation of the ancient "enigmas", which give an indication of some type of divine war. This is hinted at in the writing of the Greeks, Pherecydes, Heraclitus and Homer. It is contained in the mysteries which relate the war of the Titans and Giants with the gods, and in those of the Egyptians which tell of Typhon, Horus and Osiris and in other writings (VI. 42–43). The concept of the Son of God is, similarly, a misunderstanding of the ancient cosmogonical concept. The ancients referred to the world as God's child and demigod because it had originated from Him. The Christian concept of Jesus and the ancient child of God are very much the same.

Misunderstanding the Judaeo-Christian account of the creation of the world and of man, and of his expulsion from paradise, Celsus states that the Christian cosmogony is a ridiculous story written primarily for amusement and comparable to the writings of the poets of the Old Comedy (VI. 49). Confusing the true Christian teaching on creation with an unidentified heretical notion, Celsus asks if a creator opposed to the supreme God created the world and all within it, why did the latter lend to such a Creator the power to create; why did he give him the Spirit and then ask for it to be returned? Why does He constantly seek to destroy the works of the Creator; and why does He draw to Him as His children all those who have been condemned by their Creator father? What impressive God desires to be the father of sinners condemned by another (VI. 51–53). However, Celsus continues, if the Christians believe that this world is the creation of the supreme God, why does God create evil; why is he unable to persuade

52

and admonish men; why does he repent when the individuals whom he has created become wicked and ungrateful; and why does he find fault with His own creation and threaten and destroy his own offspring (VI. 53)? It appears that the Christians have no real understanding of the origin and nature of the world and of mankind. Thus, they believe the absurd tales written by Moses and the prophets (VI. 49–50).

Continuing the discussion of the Christians corruption of the ancient traditions, Celsus states that the Christian teaching of non-violence even when injured, and Jesus' saying of turning the other cheek, is an adaptation of a Platonic statement in the *Crito*. In this, Socrates states that man should never do wrong nor take revenge even when wronged (VII. 58).[16] He approves of the Christian attitude against idolatry, but claims that it is no different from that of the Scythians, Libyans, Syrians, Persians, and other impious and lawless nations. However, he strongly disapproves of their dishonor and disrespect to images and statues dedicated to the gods. The Christians, he claims, will not honor these images because they believe that they are dedicated to demons and not to gods, and that one who worships God should not serve demons. Yet, they themselves worship Jesus, who is neither a god, nor a demon, but a corpse (VII. 62–68).

Although Celsus strongly disapproved of the Christians' plagarizing and corruption of the ancient traditions, it was Christianity's central idea, the Incarnation, to which he most strongly objected and which constituted the main point of contention with Christianity. According to him, the Incarnation was an absurd and disgraceful notion. It was due to the Judaeo-Christian misconception of God as one who irrationally interferes throughout the course of history, and one who whimsically created the world and will destroy it by fire with the exception of a select few (IV. 10–11; 23; V. 14).

However, if as tradition claims, God is good, beautiful and blessed and possesses these qualities in perfection, a descent to the material world implies a change, a change from good to bad, from beautiful to shameful, from happiness to misfortune, and from what is best to what is most wicked. Since God is immortal and immutable, he is not subject to alteration. Thus, He is not able to undergo this change (IV. 14).[17] If it is impossible for God to change, then those who see him in a mortal body have been deceived by him to think that he has changed. This is not necessary of God, for He has no need for deceit (IV. 18). In addition, if there is the slightest change in the world, if God left his throne, everything would be overturned; the slightest change would produce chaos (IV. 5). Moreover, what purpose would the descent of God serve? God is knowledgeable of all that happens on earth and can remedy what is wrong by divine power. There is no need to send someone especially born for this purpose (IV. 3). To claim that God descended because He was unknown among man and came to be known, is to attribute to God a very mortal ambition. It is to make God act like a man who has come into wealth and is showing off. (IV. 6). Furthermore, why would God after numerous years of inactivity decide to judge humanity? Didn't He care before? If God, like Zeus in the comic poet, awakened after a long sleep and wanted to deliver the human race from evils, why did he send his Spirit down to one individual, in one small corner of the earth. He ought to have breathed it into many bodies throughout the world. In order to raise a laugh in the theatre, the comic poet wrote that Zeus sent Hermes to the Athenians and the Spartans. It is more ludicrous to have the Son of God sent to a corrupt race like the Jews instead of to an inspired nation like the Chaldeans, Egyptians, Persians or Indians (VI. 78, 80).

Celsus' Platonic concept of evil and his understanding of God's relation to the world and all created beings, led him to maintain that the purpose of the Incarnation is untenable. If, as he believed, everything revolves in a circuit; if evils could neither increase or decrease, then redemption is impossible; moral evil cannot be cured or eliminated (IV. 64–70).[18] Moreover, as he maintains, man is not superior to the irrational creatures. In fact, many animals are superior to man. God cares for each created being and never abandons anyone. He appoints to each his proper destiny and place for the good of the whole universe. God neither threatens his creatures, nor becomes angry at men anymore than at apes or mice. The doctrine of the Incarnation assumes a divine element and superior dignity in man which is incompatible with his real insignificance, as Celsus believed (IV. 74–99).[19] Thus, Celsus contended, there is no sufficient cause or adequate end for the descent of God. Therefore, the claim of Christianity to be a universal religion based on the coming of God to earth is irrational and absurd.

After presenting the various objections to Christianity, Celsus attempts to show the Christians a better way to understand the divine truths and to salvation. God, he claims, can be seen and understood not by the senses but by turning away from the world of sense and looking upward with the mind, by turning away from the flesh and raising the eyes of the soul. One is guided along the path of truth by inspired poets, wise men and philosophers. Deceivers and sorcerers who court phantoms should be avoided, and one must not blaspheme as phantoms those who prove themselves to be gods while worshiping Jesus, a man more wretched than the phantoms, who is not even a phantom anymore but a dead man (VII. 36). Divine men and philosophers seek the truth by means of synthesis or analysis or analogy, and try to give to man an intelligible concept of the First Being or God (VII. 42). The divine spirit, he continues, which the Christians believe descended to foretell the divine truths, is the very spirit which inspired wise men of ancient times to proclaim the many excellent doctrines through the ages. It is not novel with the Christians (VII. 45). However, he concludes, since the Christians had a desire to introduce a new doctrine, it would have been much better if they had chosen some other individual to give their homage, someone among the many ancients who has died an illustrious death and who is sufficiently distinguished to merit a divine legend (VII. 53).

IV. Controversy on the Relations of Christianity to National Life

Not only were many of the Christian beliefs philosophically untenable and absurd, but the movement itself was creating a rift in the already weakened Empire. Celsus viewed Christianity as a mass religious and political apostasy, a deliberate abandonment of all traditions. The strict adherence of the Christians to monotheism forbade them to worship anything other than the one Supreme God. Thus, making it impossible for them to worship the emperor or his genius, honor the traditional gods, participate in the local sacrificial ceremonies, and acknowledge the symbols of Roman power. Moreover, their pacifism would not allow them to bear arms nor to participate in the Empire's wars (VIII. 73). As Celsus charges them, the Christians walled themselves off from the rest of mankind, even refusing to accept public office, and in general being extremely reserved on anything of a political nature (VIII. 2, 75). The Christians on the other hand, firmly believed that they better served society by serving the Church (VIII. 73–75).

The attitude of the Christians appeared to the rulers and masses of the Empire as a deliberate expression of disloyalty, and a threat to the safety of the State. To the Romans, the security and well-being of the Empire was intimately connected with the pagan religion. They believed that the gods would protect the interests of the Empire in return for the allegiance of its inhabitants. To violate this belief meant either that the offended gods had to be appeased or the violators punished. As a result, the Christians were frequently tortured and persecuted. Nonetheless, they were so loyal to their faith, that they would rather suffer punishment than deny it. Yet despite the dangers from the State, the Christian movement continued to expand and to attract individuals from all walks of life. Celsus feared that the continued growth of this uncooperative, obstinate body would be disastrous to the Empire, especially at a time when it was in grave danger from the barbarians. His grave concern for the safety of the State is evident in the closing statements of his treatise where he implores the Christians not to forget loyalty and support to the emperor and the Roman State in their devotion to the new social order within the State. He appeals to the Christians to help the emperor and cooperate with him in maintaining justice and preserving the laws and religion. The Christians, he states, ought not to disbelieve Homer who long ago proclaimed, "Let there be one ruler, one King."[20] He states that if everyone acted as the Christians do, there would be nothing to prevent the emperor from being abandoned, and left solitary and desolate. Then, the affairs of the world would fall into the hands of the most lawless and savage barbarians. The Christian worship and its true wisdom would disappear forever from mankind (VIII. 63–75). Only through a united effort and a united people could the dangers threatening the Empire be averted. Thus, Celsus' main concern about Christianity was its profound social and political conse-quences, consequences which he considered most destructive to the Roman Empire.

V. Origen's Defense of Christianity

Origen strongly objected to Celsus' statement that the Chris-tian doctrines have been borrowed and corrupted from the Greek writings, especially Plato, and are basically inferior. As an apologist, he considered it most important to maintain both the antiquity and the venerable character of the Christian writings or scriptures. He strongly asserts that no Christian dogma, and no particular saying in scripture has been bor-rowed from the Greek writers, and attempts to show that they are original, superior and diviner than those of the Greek thinkers (VI. 12, 15). Moses and the prophets, whom Celsus claims borrowed from the ancient thinkers, are older than the men from whom they are alleged to have borrowed, and lived even before the invention of the Greek alphabet (IV. 21; VI. 7, 47). It is true that the apostles of Christ were much later than Plato, but it is absurd to think that uneducated fisherman like Peter and John based their doctrines of God on a misunderstanding of the teachings in Plato's epistles (VI. 7). Rather it appears that the similarity between Plato's doctrine of God and that of the Old Testament might be due to Plato's familiarity with the Old Testament scriptures (IV. 39). Nor are the Christian writings inferior to Greek philosophy.

Origen acknowledges that philosophy and Christianity have several truths in common, and that philosophy served as a valuable preparation for revealed theology. The Bible does not discourage the study of philosophy, but encourages it as a valuable tool for understanding the truth of God's revelation (I. 13; III. 47; VI. 7–8). However, a comparison of the common doctrines reveals Christianity to be far superior to Greek philosophy. Philosophy is neither essential nor adequate for the understanding of God's truths (III. 58; VI. 13ff.). This can only be accomplished through the wisdom disclosed through the Holy Scriptures (III. 58). Moreover, the superiority of the Christian writings can be attested by their moral force (I. 18). The most profound speculations of the philosophers were only theories and bore no fruit. Their theorizing and philosophical discourses composed in beautiful prose did not help their readers or even the writers to advance in piety. None of the ancient philosophers ever succeeded in implanting his version of the truth among the various nations, or for that matter among the majority of individuals in a single nation; nor did the philosophic writings lead to the abandonment of polytheism (V. 43; VI. 1–5). However, the simple words and style of the divine Scriptures, which Celsus calls "vulgar," have had the power to inspire and transform multitudes from vice to virtue and cowards to such bravery that they do not even fear death for the sake of their beliefs (III. 68). This power of the Scriptures is, according to Origen, the main proof of the truth of Christianity and its writings. Contrary to philosophy which can be read, understood and appreciated only by the educated, the Scriptures have a message and meaning for all, from the most enlightened to the most uneducated, in accordance with each individual's capacity to receive and understand its doctrines (VII. 41).

Celsus' attack on the Church as a divided group composed only of uneducated and dishonorable individuals from whom is demanded an irrational, unreasoning faith is, according to Origen, unfounded. He agrees that divisions and divergences of opinion exist within Christianity, but they existed from the very beginning. Even among the disciples or eyewitnesses of Jesus, there was never absolute unity of beliefs. There were always certain varieties of interpretation, even about the resurrection. However, such divergencies should not be considered a criticism of Christianity, but an indication of the importance of its principles and its benefit to life. There is no existing, serious teaching, essential to mankind, that has not caused different interpretations or sects. This is true of the science of medicine and of philosophy. Medicine is useful and necessary to man, and there are many problems and discussions among individuals in the field concerning the method and cure of an illness. As a result, several sects are found both among the Greeks and barbarians who profess to study the science. The same is true of philosophy which professes to possess the truth and knowledge of realities, instructs man how he ought to live, and tries to teach what is beneficial to mankind. These problems allow for great diversity of opinion, and thus have given rise to many philosophical sects. Moreover, Judaism with its variety of interpretations of the Mosaic writings and the sayings of the prophets, has caused many sects to arise within it. Since Christianity also appeared to mankind as something worthy of serious attention, not only to the uneducated, as Celsus believes, but also to the Greek scholars, it too gave rise to various sects. The divergence of thought within Christianity was due to the serious attempt of several learned men to understand the truths of Christianity. The result was that many interpreted the divine Scriptures differently and disagreed with one another (III. 11–12). Thus, according to Origen, the various sects within Christianity, and in particular the various Gnostic groups to which he continually alludes, arose not because of factions and love of strife, but because of the intellectual interest and curiosity of the Greek mind in the Christian truths.

However, he does not accept the Gnostic heresies. He condemns and does not consider as Christians any group that has introduced into the religion strange innovative ideas that are not in harmony with the traditional doctrines established by Jesus (V. 61).

Continuing his discussion on the various divisions in the Church, Origen states that no one would avoid medicine or hate philosophy because of the various sects within each. Similarly, the sacred books of Moses and of the prophets should not be despised because of the various interpretation which gave rise to the Jewish sects. Why then should anyone criticize Christianity because of its sects? He concludes his remarks with a quotation from St. Paul, "For there must also be heresies among you that they which are approved may be made manifest among you."[21] A qualified man of medicine is one who knows well all the existing medical sects and who, after careful examination of each, chooses the best with an open mind. The individual well advanced in philosophy has knowledge of and training in the various schools of thought and follows that school which has convinced him of its reasonableness. Similarly, claims Origen, the best and wisest Christian is one who has carefully studied and analyzed all the Jewish and Christian sects (III. 11–13; V. 61).

To the accusation that Christianity seeks only the ignorant and dishonorable, Origen answers that in Christianity, as everywhere else, the uneducated far out-number those that have been trained in rational thinking (I. 27). However, the Church does not seek out only the uneducated. Wisdom has a high priority in the Church. Origen quotes numerous passages from the Scriptures that stress the importance of wisdom. Christianity, he claims, is so desirous of wise and educated men that in its writings it has expressed certain truths in enigmas, parables and problems for the purpose of training its believers and making them wise (III. 45). It seeks the intelligent minds that can understand and interpret these hidden truths (III. 74). According to Origen, education is the path to virtue and to knowledge of God. To be intelligent, educated, and to have studied the best doctrines is a major help in attaining knowledge and understanding of God (III. 49, 72; VI. 14). It is not possible for an individual who has not been trained in human wisdom to acquire understanding of the more divine truths. However, human wisdom is only a means of education for the soul, divine wisdom is the ultimate end. In comparison with divine wisdom, human wisdom is mere foolishness (VI. 13–14). Moreover, when the Church calls for the "uneducated, slaves and ignorant," as Celsus claims, it does not necessarily mean those without education. The term is often used in a moral sense, and applies to those who acknowledge, invoke and ask aid from powerless or lifeless objects, and ignore or turn away from the true God. The most simple of the Christians has been freed from this condition of ignorance (VI. 14).

What is true in Celsus' remark is that the Church welcomes both the educated and wise, and the uneducated (III. 48). The Gospel is a universal document by means of which the Church seeks to reach all individuals, even the young and the slaves, how they may obtain freedom of thought. The Christian teachers admit that they seek to cure the souls of both the wise and the unwise, so that, as far as it is possible, they may earnestly seek more understanding. However, this tendency to seek to bring men to a better life is not limited only to Christians. Philosophers exhort young men to abandon an evil life for better things. They encourage slaves and stupid men to study philosophy so that they might pursue virtue. Yet no one would consider condemning them. Why then, asks Origen, should the Christians be criticized for their desire to heal every rational soul by the medicine of the Logos and reconcile it with God the Creator of all (III. 54)? Moreover, it is foolish to say, as Celsus does, that because there are so many Christians that are uneducated, the educated or intelligent individuals tend to avoid its doctrines. It is equivalent to saying that no intelligent individual would obey the laws of Solon, Lycurgus, or any other law giver, because of the multitude of the uneducated who live by their laws. Just as these and other law-givers created laws that would be most beneficial for those governed, so God enacted laws through Jesus for all men everywhere to lead them to a better existence (III. 73).

Nor, claims Origen, is Celsus' accusation that the Church prefers only the morally weak and dishonorable correct. The Church calls the sinners or those sick in the soul in order to cure them. It also summons the healthy to a knowledge and understanding of the deeper spiritual truths. At first it summons individuals to be cured, the sinners to come and learn doctrines that will teach them not to sin, the unwise to hear doctrines that will implant in them understanding, children to advance to a manly character, and the unhappy to be made blessed. Then, when each has progressed and increased in purity and has begun to live a better life. then they are summoned to the more mystical doctrines (III. 59–60). If one were to consider Christians as a whole, one would find a considerable number of converts from evil ways. In fact, no evil persons exist among the so-called true Christians. At least they are not among the individuals who attend the common prayers. They are excluded if they do come. To find a wicked person among such a group is a rare occurrence (IV. 27). This is due to the methods used to establish high moral standards in the adherents.

Before anyone is admitted into the Christian community, they must first go through a period of probation and sufficiently show their desire to live a better life. When admitted, if an individual falls into sin, especially the sin of licentiousness, they are driven out of the community of common prayer. They can be readmitted at a later time, after they have shown a change of conduct and have undergone a long period of probation. Their probation period is much longer than the one they had to undergo when they first joined the community. However, although readmitted to the community, these individuals are excluded from any Church office or administration (III. 51).

Origen does not deny Celsus' charge of the Christian blind faith. However, he attempts to show that this is not the most desirable approach to faith, but is sometimes a necessity due the limited mental abilities of individuals. It is justified by the moral reforms that it effects. If every individual had nothing else to do but devote himself to the rational investigation of the Christian truths, this method would be advocated and adopted as the only one. The Christian faith is much dependent on speculative thought. There are numerous enigmatic passages both in the Old and New Testament that have symbolic meanings and afford great scope for investigation (I. 9). Presenting various examples from the Scriptures, Origen points out that to exalt irrational faith above reasoned knowledge and investigation is contrary to the teachings of the Scriptures (III. 46). However, either because of the necessities of life or weaknesses inherent in individuals, few are able to spend their time in the investigation of the Christian doctrines. Therefore, it is better for the multitude to believe in the Christian doctrines blindly until they can devote themselves to the study of rational arguments. In this way, they will be morally reformed rather than wallow in evil (I. 9).

Both the simple faith and prayers of thanksgiving of the uneducated and those of the educated, rational pious are equally accepted by God (VII. 46). The Gospel is put before each individual in a form suited to his character and condition. Some are only exhorted to believe, since they are incapable of anything more. However, with others, every effort is made to teach them by means of rational arguments (VI. 10).

Christians should not be condemned because of their blind faith, as it is not exclusive to them. When an individual decides to join a school of philosophy, he does not do so after a careful examination for or against the different philosophers or philosophical schools. He joins either because he had been influenced by the arguments of a particular teacher, or he believes that some one school is better than the rest. Thus, it is from an unreasoning or irrational impulse that one becomes a Stoic, or an Epicurean, or a Platonist, or a follower of some such philosophical school. If individuals can believe in a particular founder of a school or sect and not be criticized or condemned, why can't men believe in the supreme God and in Jesus who has taught men to worship God alone? Moreover, all human life depends on blind faith. Nobody marries, travels, has children, or tills his fields wlthout hoping for the best. It is this faith or belief that things will turn out for the best that enables man to take risks even when the result is uncertain. If it is hope and faith in the future that maintains life together, is it not more reasonable to put ones faith in God who created all these things (I. 10–11)?

Concerning Celsus' attacks on the person and work of Christ, and his allegation that his divinity was fiction or an invention, Origen answers that it is extremely difficult and often impossible to substantiate any story as historical fact and to prove its truthfulness. He cites as an example the account of the Trojan War. Suppose someone claimed that the Trojan War never occurred because of some of the impossible events in the story; how could it be substantiated that the war really happened? The fair minded reader of the Trojan event will guard against deceit by deciding what should be accepted as truth, what should be explained allegorically, and what has been written simply to please certain individuals. The same holds true with regard to the events about Jesus in the Gospels. Christianity, claims Origen, does not demand an unreasonable, irrational faith, but that the readers of the Gospels maintain an open mind, investigate carefully, and attempt to understand with what purpose or spiritual meaning each event was written (I. 42). There is nothing in the Gospels that is fictitious, spurious or wicked. This is inferred by the piety and good conscience which the writers of the Gospels show in their writings. Moreover, men do not endure hardships and even death for fictitious stories as Jesus' followers did because of his words. From this it is clear to anyone with an open mind that Jesus' disciples were convinced of the truth of what they had recorded, and truly believed that he was the Son of God (II. 10; III. 39). The writers of the Gospels were men who were unaware of the subtle sophistries of the Greeks or the art of forensic rhetoric. Thus, they could not have invented such stories which had the power to bring men to believe and to live in conformity with these beliefs. Jesus selected simple, uneducated men to teach his doctrine, in order that there would not be any possibility of suspicion of plausible sophism. Thus, it should be clear to any intelligent individual that the writers of the Gospels were endowed with divine power which has accomplished far more than could be accomplished by Greek argument or rhetoric (I. 62; III. 39).

The Gospel, continues Origen, has a proof of its own, more divine than any writing based on Greek dialectics. This more divine proof the apostle Paul calls a "demonstration of the spirit and of power."[22] Of the spirit because of the prophecies, and especially those which refer to Christ, which are capable of producing faith in anyone who reads them; of power because of the miracles which have been performed and can be proven to have happened by many arguments as well as by the fact that traces of them still remain among those who live their lives according to the maxims of the gospels (I. 2).

Celsus' slanders about Jesus' birth are untrue. Origen states that the divine spirit or Logos, that the Christians call the Son of God, became incarnate and was born of the Virgin Mary. This conception did not pollute the spirit anymore than the rays of the sun become defiled and lose their purity when they come into contact with odorous bodies or objects (VI. 73). Nor is there any truth to the charge of adultery stated by Celsus. It is contrary to reason to think that one who performed such great deeds, and who was able to persuade mankind, both Greeks and barbarians to turn away from evil and to live in a manner acceptable to the Creator, should be born in a disgraceful manner rather than a miraculous one (I. 32). If, according to the Greek philosophers whom Celsus often quotes, a soul receives a body in accordance with its merits, then Jesus' soul, which lived a more useful life on earth than most men, would require a body superior to all others (*Ibid.*) Moreover, if souls are sent into bodies of varying degrees of rationality, why could there not be a certain soul, such as Jesus', that takes a body which is entirely miraculous, which has something in common

65

with all men in order to be able to live with them, but which also has something unique, so that the soul may remain continuously untouched by sin (I. 33). The off-spring of an adulterous affair would have been a fool, a teacher of licentiousness, unrighteousness and other evils, and not a teacher of self-control, righteousness and other virtues (*Ibid.*).

Having assumed a human body, Jesus lived and died in accordance with the human nature that he had assumed, and in accordance with human methods and arrangements. Origen stresses that Jesus was a "composite being", at once both human and divine (I. 66). In the incarnation, the immortal God, the Logos, assumed a mortal body and a human soul (IV. 15; III. 29). This resulted in the union of the soul of Jesus with the divine Logos, and formed a single personality. However, this oneness did not cause the deification of Jesus' body nor the absolute circumscription of the Logos. Jesus' visible body was not God. Therefore, it was not God who was crucified and died, but a man (II. 9, 16). In fact, the person and essence of the divine being in Jesus is quite a different matter from that of his human aspect. No one, not even the simplest, most uneducated Christian would say that the divine Logos, or the truth, or life had died (VII. 16). Therefore, Jesus' human actions cannot be condemned.

For this reason Jesus' flight from Herod cannot be considered disgraceful, as Celsus claims. He was led away by those individuals who were raising him, after they had been directed to do so by an angel of God. His flight was not from fear of death, but in order to bring help to others by continuing to live until the time when it was expedient for him to die a human death, which brought a certain benefit to mankind (I. 61, 66). Similarly, Jesus ate, drank and suffered as a human. His sufferings were real. If he only appeared to have suffered human agonies, how could he be a pattern to those who were later to endure religious persecutions (I. 25). Thus, by insisting that the incarnation was a real assumption of a human nature which included some confinement of the divine attributes and

66

the ascription of human factors and relations, Origen dispels Celsus' much repeated objections of the Christian God fleeing, thirsting, suffering and dying.

In response to Celsus' statement that foreknowing all that happened Jesus could have avoided his betrayal and death, Origen states that his pain and suffering could not be avoided. Apart from the fact that his death was a benefit to the whole of mankind, it was also a necessary part of his mission. Just as he was the example to man of how they ought to live, it was necessary that he should be an example to them of how they ought to die for the sake of religion (II. 16). Moreover, others throughout history have not avoided death for their principles. Socrates could have avoided taking the hemlock, but he preferred to die in accordance with the principles of his philosophy rather than live in contradiction to them. The same is true of the Spartan general Leonidas who died with his men at Thermopylas, and St. Paul when he went to Jerusalem, although he knew what would happen to him there. Likewise, many could avoid death by denying Christianity, but voluntarily choose death (II. 17). Furthermore, Origen asserts, Celsus' accusation that Jesus, by foreknowing his disciples treacherous actions and not thwarting them, is guilty of conspiracy, is foolish and illogical. It does not follow that because Jesus correctly predicted the actions of his disciples he was responsible for their impiety and wicked conduct. These things happened as being possible, and since they happened, it proves that Jesus foretold them. The truth about the future, claims Origen, is decided by actual occurrences (II. 19).

To Celsus' claim that Jesus' divinity is not unique but has many parallels in history, Origen answers that the most important proof of Jesus' true divinity is his work and the influence he has exerted on future generations. In particular, the moral transformation that has taken place in the world because of him. No other miracle worker or so-called divine man can make this claim. This transformation could not have been effected by Jesus without divine power. Origen considered the moral force introduced and obtained by Christianity in the world as its pre-eminent factor and he stresses it frequently throughout the work.

It is Jesus' divine power that has caused many dissolute to become temperate, the superstitious to become pious, evil passions to be checked, and savage natures to become gentle (I. 64; IV. 5). These are all clear indications of Jesus' true divinity. Moreover, Jesus' divinity continues to be evident in the world through traces of the Holy Spirit that are still preserved among the Christians. The power of the Holy Spirit has converted many to Christianity in spite of themselves. It is as if a spirit suddenly transformed their minds from a hatred of the gospel to a readiness to die for it (I. 46). Jesus' power and influence continues to grow through the progress and development of Christianity and its adherents. According to Origen, Christianity has exercised greater and more intense influence in the world than any other hitherto known religion or philosophical thought. Christianity is at once both universal and individual, a spiritual energy created by Jesus that continues. This, Origen feels, is a most definite indication and proof of Jesus' divinity.

Origen continues his proof of Jesus' divinity by refuting Celsus' attacks of Jesus' miracles. He claims that the miracles and deeds performed by Jesus prove him to be "the power of God".[23] In no way can they be compared with those of sorcerers or heroes of Greek mythology, as Celsus claims. First of all, Jesus did not perform his miracles merely to show his own powers as sorcerers and magicians do. Secondly, a sorcerer does not employ his tricks to summon the onlookers to moral reform, to bring them to the fear of God, nor persuade them to live as individuals who will be judged by God. Sorcerers don't do any of these things because they neither have the ability nor the desire to reform men. They themselves are shameful and notorious sinners. However. Jesus used his miracles to persuade those who saw the happenings to moral reformation and to live in conformity with the will of God. Jesus' miracles are differentiated from all others by their moral aim. In fact, Jesus' life, doctrine and miracles all had the same aim, to teach men to live their lives and perform every action with reference to the will of the supreme God. All this is proof enough that Jesus cannot be compared with sorcerers, but rather he was God who had been incarnated for the benefit of the human race (I. 68).

The same reasons can be used against Celsus' comparison between Jesus and Asclepius, Heracles, Dionysus and others. Most of their miracles were either caused to be written by demons or, if they did occur, it was through the operation of a demon. No proof or evidence has been given that the miracles of the Greeks actually happened. In fact, the so-called miracles of Greek mythology appear to have been only marvels with no lofty aim or purpose, and no benefit to mankind. Moreover, there is no evidence that the men who performed these marvels had any claim to divinity. What is evident is that, although they performed some good things, they are known to have performed countless actions contrary to right reason. Their life was inconsistent with any divinity of character. This is not so with Jesus. The miracles that he wrought were only a means to an end, to bring men to a better way of life which leads to fellowship with God. That end is a testimony to their reality. In addition, they are consistent with his life and teachings. They cannot be judged alone, but as components of what is considered to be a consistent whole (III. 28–34, 42).

Origen uses similar arguments to refute Celsus' statement that Jesus' resurrection and ascension had many parallels in Greek history. There is no basis for comparison between the heroes of history and Jesus, for there is no clear proof that these men actually died. It is possible that these men might have merely disappeared from the eyes of men for a period of time and then returned again to the individuals whom they had left. Jesus, on the other hand, was crucified and his body put to rest before all the Jews. In fact, his death on the cross might have been made a public event so that no one would be able to say that he had deliberately disappeared from the sight of men, appeared to die but did not really do so, then reappeared and told the portentous tale that he had risen from the dead (II. 56). Just as his suffering was real and not merely apparent, so was his death and resurrection (II. 16; III. 43).[24]

That Jesus' resurrection was merely an imaginary appearance of a hallucinating woman, Mary Magdalene, Origen answers that the Gospels tell of his appearance to many individuals. He continues that Jesus' resurrection was the greatest of all miracles and follows along with all the prophecies that had been made about him in the Old Testament. Jesus' body at the time of the resurrection was in an intermediate state, between the solidity of the body before the passion and an unclothed bodiless soul.[25] This explains why he was able to enter the room where his disciples were gathered, after the doors had been shut (II. 62). Such appearances are substantiated by the teachings of Plato[26] (II. 60, 61). Jesus' appearance to his disciples was not a mere illusion. This is proven by their actions. If the disciples did not actually see Jesus after he arose from the dead, and if they were not convinced that there was something divine about him, why were they willing to suffer as he did, to face danger boldly and leave their homes to fulfill his will by teaching the doctrines which he had committed to them (I. 31)? How could a mere phantom, or vision, as Celsus considers Jesus' appearance after the resurrection, have such a great effect on man, convert the souls of so many of them and implant in them the conviction that they ought to live according to the dictates of God, who will be their judge (VII. 35)?

Celsus asks why Jesus did not disappear from the cross or appear openly before all. This statement, claims Origen, is similar to those made by foolish men against Providence, men who believe that the world would be better if it had been made according to their concepts. However, when examined, their ideas either describe a world worse than the one that exists, or they are found to desire things which are intrinsically impossible. In either case, they are ridiculous (II. 68). If Christ had disappeared suddenly from the cross, Celsus would have wondered why he didn't disappear before his passion rather than after the crucifixion. Moreover, it was not feasible that

Jesus disappear physically from the cross. The purpose of his crucifixion and death also involved his burial. Just as all the other events recorded to have happened to Jesus cannot be judged in isolation, so the resurrection must be regarded as a part of the whole experience having a symbolic meaning (II. 69).

Jesus did not appear to all after his resurrection out of kindness to those who had treated him contemptuously, lest they should be smitten with blindness as the wicked men of Sodom.[27] He appeared only to those who were able to receive his divine power, and according to the capacity of each (II. 67). Jesus was able to be seen by all, and he appeared quite often to the crowds before this crucifixion. However, after his passion, he appeared only to those who were fit to behold him (II. 66). According to Origen, the purpose of the resurrection was to show that the Logos is alive and guides all those who are willing to follow. After the resurrection, Jesus appeared to reveal the deeper truths of the next stage of progress to those who were not capable of understanding them at the time of their conversion to Christianity (V. 58). For Origen, the resurrection was God's promise to mankind of the eternal life through knowledge of him and of his truths.

Celsus accuses Jesus of being a failure as a teacher, a destitute wanderer teaching doctrines borrowed and corrupted from the Greek philosophers and who, while he lived, could not even convince his own disciples. The few followers that he succeeded in acquiring were found to be faithless. Origen answers these attacks by maintaining that, contrary to Celsus' remarks, Jesus' teaching had no equal. In fact, it was his great popularity as a teacher that roused against him the envy of the chief priests, elders and scribes (II. 39). Thousands, men, women and children, were persuaded and followed him to the deserts. Some were convinced by his well-reasoned arguments which he always expressed in words appropriate for his audience, others were convinced by his miracles, and still others by both these things (II. 39, 43; III. 10). Frequently, his audiences were so great in number that only the desert could hold such a multitude (II. 46). Therefore, it is a falsehood to say that he could not even convince his own disciples. It is true that, initially, his disciples displayed some degree of human cowardice. However, they never gave up their belief that he was the Christ, the Son of God, and finally, they died for his teachings (II. 39, 45). From the very beginning, Jesus' teaching had a great influence upon his listeners. It taught them to seek a life beyond everything sensible and corruptible; to live a life akin to that of God (II. 45). To claim that these teachings are borrowed and corrupted from the Greek philosophers, and in particular Plato, is absurd. Anyone with even the slightest knowledge of the facts, Christian or not, knows that Jesus could not have read or known either Plato or any other philosopher. He was born and bred among the Jews, the son of a carpenter named Joseph, and, as the Scriptures testify,[28] he had studied neither the writings of the Greeks nor the Hebrews (VI. 16). Jesus' doctrines are derived from a higher source than philosophy. They are derived from an understanding and knowledge of the supreme God the Father (VI. 17). What Celsus considers vagabondism on the part of Jesus was his desire to proclaim this knowledge everywhere, to every city and village of Judea (II. 38).

The main proof of Jesus' claims is the great progress and success of the Gospel—the teachings of Jesus. This Origen repeatedly maintains throughout the Apology. Jesus' teaching has brought about great changes among all men, in every corner of the globe. Despite countless hinderances, the Gospel continues to become even more powerful. It has won over men of every nature, every race, and of every level of society throughout the whole world of mankind. It has converted them to a better way of life, and has implanted in them a love for Christianity that they would rather die for it than renounce or forsake it. This has never been claimed for any other doctrine (I. 26, 29; II. 13; V. 62; VII. 41; VIII. 59).

Jesus has performed all this and continues to perform it, without benefit of the advantages that enable men to become famous, or distinguished, i.e., noble birth, wealthy parents, an expensive education, or citizenship of a great and famous country. As a poor country man, speaking in the simple words of the populace and proclaiming a simple message—to live in accordance with the will of God in order to enjoy communion with Him—he has been able to perform a unique and super-human task. He has instilled within men the concept of a universal empire. Origen maintains that all this is possible because of Jesus' divinity; he is "the power of God and the wisdom of the Father"[29] (I. 29; II. 79). Everything that happens is because of his divine power. Thus, Jesus cannot be classed with any heroes or national gods or demons. He has shown that he alone is divine and superior to all of them. He has taken followers from all their territories and, by means of his divine power, has caused not only men who are willing to welcome him, but also demons, gods and other invisible powers to fear him as superior or accept him in reverence as their lawful ruler (III. 36).

As previously mentioned, Celsus' primary objection to Christianity was the doctrine of the Incarnation. This he vigorously condemned as an absurd and irrational notion. To Celsus' fierce attack, Origen contends that Christianity is not the first religion to speak of a divine descent. There exist popular beliefs in most countries of gods who come down from heaven to earth either to give oracles to men or to heal them by means of oracular utterances (V. 2). Moreover, Origen con-tends, Celsus' arguments against the incarnation proceed from a lack of understanding of the true nature of God, the value of the human soul, its nature and necessary freedom of will, and of the moral results of Christianity. The attribute of change does not apply to God. He is superior to all place, and comprehends everything; there is nothing that contains God (VII. 34). Therefore, the descent of God is not a literal or topical one. It does not involve the abandonment of His throne nor any change in Him. It is God's power and divinity that came to dwell among men and care for their affairs through the man whom God willed to choose while remaining completely unchanged in essence (IV. 5, 14; V. 12). He who descended among men was "in the form of God", and because of His love of man humbled Himself that he might be accessible to man (IV. 15). He underwent no change from good to evil, for He knew no sin, nor from blessedness to misfortune, although He humbled Himself for the advantage of the human race. No one would suggest a similar degeneration of a physician whose interest and concern for man causes him to view and handle terrible things and unpleasant wounds in order that suffering may be cured. In a similar manner, the incarnated Logos, who heals the wounds of the soul, was incapable of any evil. The immortal, divine God—the Logos—although assuming a human body and a human soul, undergoes no change or transformation, but remains the same in essence. He does not suffer any of the experiences of the body or soul (IV. 15, 19). Moreover, God's coming to earth was not due to the need for God to repair His work; it was man's work that needed repair.

According to Origen, the world, as God's creation, is not evil, nor is God the cause of evil. Evil is not part of the essential nature of the material world, but is due to the rational beings—man's resistant will. It is man in the exercise of his freedom that is the cause of the moral evil and confusion that exists in the world. Evils are the actions which result from each individual's freedom of choice. Origen asserts that evil, or lack of it, is dependent on the use that man, through his reasoning faculty, makes of the images and impressions presented to him. Each individual, according to his choice, is responsible for the evils which exist in him (IV. 66–70).[30] It is for the purpose of correcting the evils in the world and preventing them from spreading further that God has revealed Himself in progressive revelations (IV. 4, 69). To assume, as Celsus does, that everything in the world revolves in a circuit, that moral evil is irremediable and redemption impossible is to admit that man does not possess free-will, that man's free-will has been annihilated—is non-existent (IV. 67).

74

The incarnation of the Logos represents God's pre-eminent act of redemption of mankind. It was not, as Celsus contends, the outcome of a sudden impulse, but the ultimate stage in a series of God's revelations. According to Origen, God has been concerned with the salvation of the souls of men since the creation of the world. In every generation, God's wisdom has descended into the souls of the pious in order that they might help their contemporaries to convert to the ways of God (IV. 7). The souls who were invested with the Divine Spirit, namely the prophets and other holy men, were rational spirits who had not fallen very far from God. They were clothed with human bodies not because of their own sins, but so that they might be of help to others who were struggling with temptation and to provide them with knowledge of the truth (VI. 7).

Origen identifies three separate major progressive revelations of God—the natural law, the Mosaic Law and the incarnation of the Logos. The natural law is the conscience or rational reasoning that is inherent in all rational beings—man, angels and sidereal spirits alike. No human being has followed this law completely. However, some men to a great extent have been guided by the law of reason. The ancient philosophers, both Greek and barbarian represent examples of men who were guided by reason. However, they had not advanced far enough; none had advanced beyond the state of polytheism to the true worship of God (V. 43; VI. 1–5; VII. 47, 49). Thus, although implanted by the Logos, the law of reason is insufficient to deliver man from sin and convert him to a more virtuous life (VI. 2). The Mosaic law, with its rules of conduct and sacrificial system, provided additional training and preparation; and for a time it helped to check the progression of sin and error. However, the ceremonial prescriptions of the Law were not sufficient to achieve the complete salvation of mankind. They had been revealed only to the Hebrews and were only symbols, a preparation for the more advanced knowledge that was to be disclosed (II. 2; V. 31; VII. 7). Finally, the Logos Himself appeared to mankind in order to show all men, not only a privileged few, the way to blessedness and union with God, which Origen considers man's ultimate goal in life. It was the Logos' greatest attempt to reconcile mankind with God by becoming the example and model for its salvation (VI. 68).

From the beginning of creation, the Logos was united with a rational spirit, a spirit which had chosen the good with unshakable resolve. At a particular time, the spirit that was joined to the Logos assumed a human body and became a human soul. Together with the human body, the soul advanced until it became divine (III. 41; IV. 15). According to Origen, the various functions and attributes of the incarnated Logos are as a ladder, by which man advances step by step from his present bodily state to pure spirit. This can be accomplished through the soul's diligent imitation of Christ and through Christ's continual help and guidance, His constant enlightment of the soul at every step of the way back to its spiritual state (VII. 32, 43–44).[31]

Unlike Celsus who considered man to be on the same level as the animals and in some respects inferior to many animals (IV. 74–98), Origen affirms man's unique position in the universe, and exalts man to a position superior to that of brute creation. Interpreting Genesis I. 26–27, he states that man's rational soul, his true being, was created in the image of God and has a certain kinship or affinity with Him unlike any of the animals (IV. 30). As an image of God, man's rational soul shares in His nature and always retains within it a spark of the Divine. Thus, unlike the animals who possess only an irrational soul, man is capable of attaining perfection or likeness to God. It is the Incarnation which has made this possible. By means of the Incarnation, God has entered into the life of humanity and has made it possible for man to obtain true union with Him. The union of the divine and the human began in Jesus. Since that time, human nature, through fellowship with the divine can become divine. This is true not only in Jesus, but in all those who believe in him, and undertake to live the kind of life which he taught. This life leads man to the recovery of his knowledge of and fellowship with God (III. 28, 41). According to Origen, the Incarnation is the deification of humanity.

VI. Christianity's Contribution to the Empire

Roman law and government was very closely associated with the Roman pagan religion. Because of this, the Christians avoided, as much as possible, any participation in the political and social life of the Empire. This elusive attitude was considered unpatriotic and as a deliberate attempt to undermine and destroy the Empire. All the political, social, economic and natural disasters were blamed on the Christians, because it was believed that their attitude had angered the Roman divinities and the gods were withdrawing their protection from the State. Celsus, as a fervent patriot, stresses the obedience to the law and the emperor and piety to the gods. He urged the Christians to change their attitude and help preserve the fatherland and the continuance and increase of its power.

In his reply to Celsus, Origen takes a cosmopolitan or universal attitude. He strongly defends the behavior of the Christians, and attempts to show that ultimately it is more beneficial to the Empire and mankind as a whole than the attitude of Celsus and other so-called patriots like him. Whereas Celsus claims loyalty and patriotism to the secular law and national gods as the paramount objective, Origen emphasizes obedience to the divine law and the universal God. In this, he reveals his Platonic influence which claimed that the goal of the State should be to spread culture and civilization rather than to increase its power.

Thus, Origen states, if the Christians fail to obey the civil laws, it is because these laws are not in harmony with the divine laws. The diversity of laws among the various cities and communities indicates that the secular laws are not in the strict sense laws, but conventional standards (VIII. 26). There are, therefore, two kinds of laws—the ultimate law of nature which is derived from God, and the written law of cities. When the written law is not contradictory to the law of God, citizens should follow it and not introduce new laws. However, when the law of nature, God's law, ordains what is contrary to the written law, reason compels that one should renounce the written law and live according to the divine law, even if in doing so it is necessary to endure dangers, shame, countless troubles and even death. Moreover, if the things that are pleasing to God differ from those which are demanded by some of the State laws, and when it is impossible to please both God and those who enforce such laws, it would be unreasonable to choose the secular laws which are not true laws and do the bidding of those who uphold these laws, and ignore those laws and actions which are pleasing to the Creator of the universe. If, questions Origen, it is generally reasonable to prefer God's law to the written law which has been established by men in opposition to the law of God, is it not even more important to obey the laws which concern the worship of God (V. 37)?

It is the Christians' total loyalty and obedience to the universal God that prevents them from paying homage or seeking to gain the favor of the civil rulers. In his urging to the Christians, Celsus remarks, "What harm would there be if, along with the worship of their God, the Christians would also attempt to gain the favor of the earthly rulers and emperors. These individuals also hold their position through the instrumentality of gods" (VIII. 63). Origen replys that the Christians give loyalty and obedience only to the one supreme God. It is only His favor that they seek through prayer and the practise of every virtue. For just as a moving body is followed by the movements of its shadow, so it follows that when one has the favor of God, he also has the good will of all the angels and spirits that are dear to God (VIII. 64). Moreover, Christians avoid ingratiating themselves with Kings or other men if their favor is to be won by murders, licentious acts or savagery; by blaspheming God; or by any servile expressions of flattery. These things are alien to brave and noble men who, together with the other virtues, desire to possess courage which is the greatest of all virtues (VIII. 65).

However, Origen continues, although Christians are resolved not to disobey the law and word of God, they are not so foolish as to stir up the wrath of an emperor or governor which will bring upon them sufferings, tortures and even death (VIII.

65). Christians are loyal subjects, because they are the followers of Jesus who is the author of peace, not of sedition (VIII. 14; V. 33). Although they refuse to bear arms for the emperor, they are more effective to him by their divine help, by putting on the whole armor of God. This they do in obedience to the command of the apostle Paul who exhorts the Christians to pray, make supplications, intercessions and thanksgivings for all men, for emperors and all who are in authority.[32] In fact, the more pious an individual is, the more effective he is in helping the emperor—more so than the soldiers who go out into the lines and kill as many enemy troops as they are able (VIII. 73).

Christians are very much like the priests and wardens of the pagan temples of the gods. These individuals are not summoned to fight, in order that they may offer the customary sacrifices to the Roman so-called gods with unstained hands and pure from murders. The Christians fight as priests and worshippers of God. They keep their hands pure and strive for those who fight for a righteous cause and for the emperor who rules in righteousness by their prayers to God, so that everything which is opposed and hostile to what is righteous may be over-thrown. Moreover, by means of their prayers, they destroy all demons who stir up wars, violate oaths and disturb the peace. They cooperate for the common good by teaching men not to be led by pleasures that are injurious to the State. Although Christians do not become fellow-soldiers with the emperor, they fight more on his behalf by serving as a special army of piety that fights not with weapons but with prayers through their intercessions to God (VIII. 73).

The Christians cannot participate in the public life of the country in the way that Celsus requests. In each city, they recognize another national organization—a divine country, the church of God, which was created by the Logos of God. The rulers of this commonwealth are strong in judgement and pure in their way of life. They are appointed because of their great humility, and their reluctance to take on hastily the responsibilities of the church of God, and not because of their love for power. These rulers govern perforce, they are compelled by the great King, whom Christians believe is the Son of God, the divine Logos. They know only one law, the law of God and rule in accordance with it. However, because they rule in accordance with the commands of God, they do not on this account profane any of the established civic laws (VIII. 75).

As citizens of the divine commonwealth, Christians must subordinate everything earthly to this citizenship, so that they might not lose it. For this reason, they sever themselves from all those that are alien to God's commonwealth. The Spartan ambassadors refused to pay homage to the Persian ambassador in spite of considerable pressure from his guards because they feared their only lord, the law of Lycurgus. Likewise the Christians who are ambassadors of Christ, a far greater and more divine embassy, will not worship any earthly ruler of any race whatsoever, no matter what pressures are imposed upon them to do so or to persuade them to denounce Christ who is superior to any earthly law (VIII. 5–6).

Thus, if Christians avoid civic responsibilities. it is not because they wish to avoid the public duties of life, but because they want to reserve their energies for a more divine and necessary service in the church of God for the sake of the salvation of all mankind. It is right that the Christians serve as leaders in the salvation of men and that they be concerned about all mankind, both for those who are within and those who are outside the Church. For those within the Church, they are concerned that they continue to live better lives every day; those who are outside it, that they may become familiar with the word of God and the divine law, and thus be united to the supreme God through the Son of God. It is through him that everyone who has been persuaded to live according to God's will in all things is united to the Divine, man's ultimate aim in life (VIII. 75). The Christians, therefore, rather than being detrimental to the Empire, supported the civil powers, in the noblest sense, by their lives, their prayers and their organization, and helped the whole of mankind to attain its ultimate goal, salvation.

Celsus, gravely concerned with the spread and continuance of this kind of thinking, argues that if Christianity became universal, if all men refused to participate in military or civic affairs, the Empire would be totally destroyed and chaos would reign. Origen replys that if Christianity prevailed throughout the world, as it was fast becoming and was certain one day to be, there would not be any savage and lawless barbarians, as Celsus feared. They too would be converted to the word of God and would be most law-abiding and humane (VIII. 68). If all Romans prayed to God together with complete agreement, God would help them overcome all their enemies. God rejoices when the rational beings are in harmony and turns away when they are in disagreement. If two or three individuals pray together in agreement for something and it is granted to them by the heavenly Father, what would happen if the whole of the Roman Empire were to agree and pray together? Origen answers that God would fight for them and their victory would be assured. It is true, as Celsus remarks, that God made these promises and others to the Jews. However, instead of being masters of the whole world, they have been left without any land or home of any kind. Origen states that the reason that God's promises to the Jews have not been fulfilled is not that God has gone back on his promise, but because the promises were made on condition that His Law be preserved and that men live in accordance with it. This the Jewish nation failed to do (VIII. 69).

Origen continues to stress that if all Romans were to become Christians, they would be superior to all their enemies. In fact, they would not even fight wars at all, since they would be protected by divine power which is reported to have preserved five entire cities for the sake of fifty righteous men.[33] The men of God are the salt of the world. They preserve the unity and solidarity of all things on earth. However, when men turn away from God, they are no longer able to hold the earthly things together, but like the salt which has lost its savor, are cast out and trodden under foot. In other words, there are wars and hostility because there are Godless men. Thus, claims

Origen, if all individuals became followers of God, there would be no need for anyone to participate in military activities. The Roman Empire would be protected and preserved by divine power (VIII. 70).

VII. The Universality of Christianity

A main feature of Origen's apology to Celsus and one which he frequently asserts is the universality of Christianity. He never ceases to insist on this feature throughout the text and to demonstrate its continuous realization. He believed that Christianity could unite all men of every race and nationality, of differing intellectual and moral characteristics by a common bond of religious belief. This concept, as is often emphasized throughout his polemic, was considered impossible and absurd by Celsus. Although he expresses the wish for a common law that would unite the inhabitants of Asia, Europe, and Libya, both Greeks and barbarians at the furthest ends of the earth, Celsus could not conceive of the possibility of a universal religion. The existence of a universal empire did not suggest the possibility of a universal religion, and he considered the notion the product of sheer ignorance (VIII. 72; V. 25ff.).

The Empire boasted many gods. Each had their duties and responsibilities alloted to them, and all were considered of equal importance. The addition of another god was considered by Celsus just that, just another god, and did not imply any notion of universalism. No god, and in particular the Christian god, could claim exclusive sovereignty within the Empire. Moreover, he believed that from the beginning of time, the different parts of the earth were assigned to different gods or overseers. It was important that the individuals of each nation observe their own traditions and practices of worship, whatever they may be, as long as they were pleasing to the god who was in charge of the nation. To abandon the traditional customs, and hence the national diety was considered an impiety (V. 25ff.).

In reply to Celsus, Origen argues that not only is a universal religion possible, but it is certain that at some point all rational beings will agree to follow one law, God's law, and all will be remodelled to the perfection of the Logos. Each individual, simply by the exercise of his freedom will choose what the Logos wills. Just as it is unlikely that any of the physical diseases would be too difficult to be healed by medical science, so also it is unlikely that any evils found in souls would be incapable of being cured by God. The Logos and the healing power within him are more powerful than any evils in the soul. This power is applied by the Logos to each individual soul according to God's will. The result of the treatment is the abolition of all evil (VIII. 72).

In fact, Origen continues, the Roman Empire has prepared the world for the coming of Christ and for the universal diffusion of Christianity. This it has done by creating a unified, peaceful world beginning with the days of Augustus onward. Jesus was born during the reign of Augustus, who had united the many kingdoms of the world into a single empire. By uniting the various kingdoms under one Roman emperor, the unfriendly attitude of the nations to one another, caused by the existence of a large number of kingdoms, was eliminated. This was God's way of preparing the nations for Jesus' teaching. The establishment of the empire made it easier for his teaching to be spread throughout the nations. It would have been even more difficult for Jesus' apostles to do what he commanded them when he said. "Go and teach all the nations."[34], if there had been many kingdoms. In addition, men everywhere would have been compelled to do military service and to fight for their different countries. This is what used to happen before the reign of Augustus, and it had happened even earlier when the occasion arose for a war between Sparta and Athens, or between other nations which fought one another. If this had happened during the time of Jesus, how could his teaching, which preaches peace and does not even permit men to take vengeance on their enemies, have had any success unless the whole world had been changed everywhere for the better and a gentler more peaceful spirit existed at the coming of Jesus (II. 30)? The prevailing international atmosphere of peace and righteousness helped to foster the spread of Christianity.

According to Origen, Christianity is already succeeding in gaining universal acceptance. By means of the incarnated Logos, it has been spread throughout most of Greece and the barbarian lands. Christianity encompasses a salvation which is offered to all men and attained through faith in God. Its aim is to bring about the moral salvation of all mankind and thus to bring all mankind into union with God. No other philosophical thought or religious cult has had sufficient power to make the truth universally known and accessible (VI. 2; VIII. 47, 59ff.). Origen likens the philosophers and other wise and religious men to the physicians who concern themselves only with the health and well-being of cultured patients, or the better class, rather than with all of man-kind. Another comparison that he makes is to the cooks that are assigned to prepare a wholesome meal for the multitude. However, they prepare food that is palatable only to the rich and better classes. The majority, having been brought up in farm-houses and in poverty, have no inclination for such food, are not able to eat it and thus, do not receive any nourishment from it (VII. 59–60). The teaching of Jesus provides health and nourishment for all. It is universal and addressed to all, even slaves, it is equally powerful over Greek and barbarian, and gains mastery over every type of human nature (II. 13). Unlike other teachings, the Gospel is a universal specific for the abolishment of evil, the healing of every rational nature and its reconciliation with God. It has the power to put an end to polytheism and to enlighten and improve each individual in accordance with his need for improvement, his knowledge, capacity and ability to receive God. Thus, it restores the rational beings back to their original unity with God. The goal which all creation is meant to achieve (VII. 33, 41–44).

84

5
Dialogue With Heraclides[1]

I. Introduction

The work *Dialogue with Heraclides* is a recent discovery. It was found among a small library of papyri in 1941 by a group of soldiers who were clearing an Egyptian quarry in Tura, south of Cairo. Until its discovery in 1941, this work of Origen was completely unknown. It appears to have been written during the latter part of the sixth century, and its exact title read: "Dialogues of Origen with Heraclides and the Bishops with him concerning the Father and the Son and the Soul". It is believed that initially the title "Dialogues of Origen: with Heraclides and the bishops with him" was placed by the original scribe at the end of the text. A later scribe added to the original title the phrase "Concerning the Father and the Son and the Soul" and placed this title at the beginning of the work.[2] From its style, vocabulary and doctrinal material, the codex appears to be an authentic work of Origen. In fact, it is believed to be Origen's most authentic piece of work.

The *Dialogue* is a complete recording of a meeting held at a synod of bishops convened to discuss what were believed to be unorthodox views on the Trinity maintained by a certain bishop Heraclides. As a recording of an actual discussion, it is a unique document among ancient and early Christian literature as a whole with the exception of the works of St. Augustine.[3] There is no indication in the text of the date and place where the meeting was held, and it is apparent that some preliminary questions of the Synod's bishops has been omitted by the scribe at the beginning of the papyrus. However, from the context of the text, it is believed that the debate probably took place somewhere in Arabia sometime between A.D. 244 and 249.[4]

From the works of Origen, as well as from the historian Eusebius, it is known that Origen often engaged in discussions of doctrinal issues under dispute,[5] and was invited by other churches to debate controversial matters of doctrine.[6] The meeting with Heraclides appears to be such a meeting. Origen was invited to Arabia to the church of Bishop Heraclides to cross-examine him on his views concerning the pre-existence of the Son, Christ and his relationship with God the Father. The Dialogue consists of three main discussions; hence perhaps the use of the plural "dialogues" in the title of the papyrus. The first and main discussion centers around Heraclides' understanding of the relationship between the Father and Son; the second consists of an objection raised by Bishop Maximus, a participant at the synod, concerning the humanity of Christ; and the third deals with the question raised by Dionysius concerning the immortality of the soul.

II. Dialogue with Heraclides

The dialogue begins with Heraclides assuring his fellow bishops of his acceptance of and belief in the pre-existence of the Logos as stated in the Gospel of John I. 1–3, and in the credal statement of the incarnation, birth, death, resurrection and second coming of Christ. Origen then interrogates Heraclides about his views of the Father/Son relationship with the aim of eliciting from him a confession of the pre-existence, independent existence and divinity of the Son. While cross-examining Heraclides, Origen develops his own views on the subject.

It seems that Heraclides objected to the expression "two gods" to express the distinction between the Father and the Son because it had polytheistic connotations. Referring to the Scriptures, Origen attempted to explain how two things can be designated as one: Adam and Eve, although two distinct

86

individuals were only one flesh (Gen. 2:24; Matt. 19:5); the righteous person is a distinct individual of a subordinate or lower nature than Christ, yet, he is one spirit with Him (1 Cor. 6:17);[7] Christ, the Son, is united to the Father as one God. Thus, claims Origen human beings can be joined to one another in flesh; a righteous individual can be joined to Christ in spirit; and Christ is united to God, the Father, in a higher more honorable way than these—in divinity; two existences united in divinity. Origen derives this understanding from Christ's statement, "I and the Father are one" (Jn. 10:30). He states that by interpreting Christ's words thus, he is able to defend both the quality of God and the divinity of Christ while also maintaining the unity of the two. In this passage, Origen considers the divinity as the unifying element between Christ, the Son, and God, the Father.[8] Therefore, Origen states, all prayers should be offered to God through Christ who is akin to and communicates with the Father because of His divinity. This does not imply two offerings to two Gods, but "to God through God".[9] There appears to have been a controversy in the church of Heraclides concerning the person to whom prayer should be addressed. Origen takes this opportunity to urge Heraclides' church to prevent any further disputes by adhering to the formula for prayers established by the Church and followed by all other churches.

Throughout the dialogue, Origen encourages Heraclides by questions and examples to agree, although somewhat reluctantly, that there are two Gods, but to add hastily, "The power is one". Thus, the discussion with Heraclides is concluded with both sides accepting the statement two gods but one power. This same phrase is used in later theology in the development of the Trinitarian doctrine: Two persons but one nature. It was important to Origen that Christ be considered as a distinct personality while still maintaining his oneness with God. To deny the independence of the Son in relation to the Father was to abolish the distinctiveness of both Father and Son; to deny the oneness of the Son in power and essence with the Father was to negate his true divinity.[10] After settling this issue, Origen proceeded to the second part of the discussion and the problem of Christ's death and resurrection.

Maximus, at an earlier stage in the discussion, seems to have raised the question concerning the reality of Christ's body, its death and resurrection. In answer to Maximus, Origen begins by professing his belief in Christ's death and resurrection, and stating that these events were proof that He had a real body and that all who believe will also rise. To assume that Christ's body was not truly a material body is, according to Origen, to deny the Church's belief in the total salvation of man. Appealing to St. Paul's tripartite division of the human compound—body, soul and spirit (I. Thess. 5:23), Origen attempts to explain what probably occurred at Christ's death and resurrection.

Interpreting St. Paul, Origen states that Christ assumed all three parts of man—body, soul and spirit—in order to redeem all three.[11] The three parts were separated at the time of the Passion: the spirit of Christ was committed temporarily to the Father; the soul parted from the body and descended into Hades; and the body was placed in the tomb. The three parts were reunited not at the moment of the resurrection but shortly afterward, as is indicated by Christ's words to Mary Magdalene on Easter morning, "Touch me not, for I am not yet ascended to the Father" (Jn. 20:17). In other words Christ did not want Mary Magdalene to touch Him before he had retrieved the spirit, which was temporarily entrusted to the Father, and thus becoming total again. It was after Christ had reclaimed His spirit and the three components of his humanity had been reunited that He appeared to His disciples.

Following this discussion, Origen proceeds to a short discussion on the equal importance of faith and correct daily conduct He states that sins, both major and minor, should be avoided and names the various sins enumerated by St. Paul (I. Cor. 6:9–10). Concluding the discourse, he asks for additional questions on any other matters of doctrine or faith.

Dionysius continues the debate by asking whether the soul and blood of man are identical. It appears that many Christians believed that this was so, and that the soul was thus material and mortal and that, at death, it remained with the body in the grave. Origen had been called to answer and refute this belief before.[12] The misunderstanding was prompted by the text of Leviticus 17:11, "The soul of all flesh is blood", which is also supported by Deuteronomy 12:23, "You shall not eat the soul with the flesh; thus take great care that you eat no blood." Interpreting the Scriptures, Origen states that man has both an inner and outer self; the soul created in the image of God, and the body made from dust.[13] Created in God's image, the soul is immaterial and superior to any material substance. However, both the inner and outer self of man have comparable parts. Thus, there is the physical blood and the blood of the interior man. The interior blood of man is man's vital power, the soul, a non-material, incorruptible, immortal entity. Frequently, the Scriptures use physical terms to describe spiritual or mystical realities. This is the case of the Leviticus text. The term "blood" is used to describe the spiritual soul which separates from the body at death.

While attempting to answer Dionysius' question, Origen was aware of the difficulty in explaining the Scriptures, especially to the uninstructed laymen who might misunderstand his teaching. Therefore, he proceeded to give a long general statement about the need to teach the truth, and the problems involved in attempting to do so.

Origen ends the conference with a further discussion on the immortality of the soul, which was prompted by Bishop Demetrius, basing his argument solely on the Scriptures. In his discussion he distinguished three kinds of death: death to sin, death to God and physical death. The soul is mortal or immortal with respect to these three deaths. In the first instance, the soul that dies to sin lives to God. This is a desired and blessed thing and a death that the soul should seek.[14] In the second, the soul that dies to God lives to sin. This is the death of the soul that has sinned grievously, and is a death that the soul can and should avoid.[15] The third death is natural death. The soul is subject to the first and second kind of death and with respect to these can be considered mortal. However, all souls are immuned to natural death. No soul can suffer this death, although those in sin desire it but cannot find it.[16] The whole discussion is concluded with Origen's exhortation to the audience to fervidly strive to live in God, and thus gain insight into the divine mysteries and ultimate union with Him.

In view of Origen's interest and careful analysis of the question of the soul's immortality in his other works,[17] his statement here is weak and pointless. Chadwick[18] believes that this might be due to Origen's desire to appear as a Biblical theologian in his doctrine of the soul rather than as a Platonist, as was implied by Bishop Demetrius. Origen's doctrine of the immortality of the soul appears not to have been fully accepted and under suspicion by some of his ecclesiastical colleagues even during his lifetime. The doctrine was totally rejected by the Church in the Second Council of Constantinople A.D. 553.

The *Dialogue* is important in providing a picture of Origen in his ecclesiastical role as theological expert called to refute heretical views of theological doctrine and in presenting his views on Trinitarian issues.

6
Practical Works

I. Introduction

Under the general heading of practical works are usually included the two ascetical treatises on practical religion, the *Exhortation to Martyrdom* and the *On Prayer*. Also included in this group is a third treatise *Peri Pascha—On Easter* or *On the Passover*, the letters of Origen addressed to individuals and the *Philocalia*.

The *Exhortation to Martyrdom* was written at Caesarea in A.D. 235 at the outbreak of the persecution of Maximinus Thrax. It is dedicated to Origen's two friends, the deacon Ambrose and the presbyter Protoctetus, both of the Church of Caesarea who were imprisoned during the persecution. The work reveals Origen's intense interest in martyrdom, a topic with which he was preoccupied since his early youth.[1] The *On Prayer* is addressed to Origen's friend and patron Ambrose and to Tatiana, a companion of Ambrose's, with the purpose of clearing up certain questions that the two had concerning prayer. It is an instructional piece of work giving instruction on prayer in general as well as an explanation of the Lord's prayer. The treatise is believed to have been written between A.D. 233 and 236. The treatise *Peri Pascha* was part of the bundle of papyri found in Tura, Egypt in 1941 and which contained the *Dialogue with Heraclides*. Preserved in fragments, the work reveals Origen's opinions on the subject of Easter, of which little information was known heretofore.[2] It is a commentary on the twelfth chapter of Exodus, which recounts the crossing of the Red Sea and the beginning of Passover. Therefore, it is appropriate to translate the title as *On the Passover*. Additional study of the fragments is needed. Their date and interpretation is still being debated by scholars.[3] Thus, these fragments will be treated summarily in this work.

Eusebius claims that Origen had written numerous letters to various individuals during his lifetime (H.E. VI. 36:3). Of these, only two are extant in their entirety. One is addressed to Julius Africanus in answer to Africanus' question concerning the authenticity of the story of Susanna in the Book of Daniel; and the other to his former pupil Gregory Thaumaturgus on the use of Greek philosophy in the study and explanation of the Scriptures. The letter to Africanus was written about A.D. 240 in Ambrose's home at Nicomedia. It was dictated by Origen and written by Ambrose. The epistle to Gregory was written about the same time, A.D. 237–243, also while Origen was in Nicomedia.

The *Philocalia* consists of a collection of extracts from Origen's writings. It was compiled by Basil the Great and Gregory Nazianzus sometime in the middle of the fourth century. About A.D. 382 it was sent to Theodore, Bishop of Tyana, and, as stated by Gregory in his dedicatory letter to Bishop Theodore, it contains the "choice thoughts" of Origen, "extracts useful for scholars".[4] The selections included in the text are primarily those which show Origen's method of explaining difficult passages of Scripture.

II. Exhortation to Martyrdom

Origen considered martyrdom as the best possible pursuit and the supreme achievement of a Christian, the best expression of gratitude to God for all that He has granted. It was "the cup of salvation",[5] best means by which an individual could attain union with the Divine, which, according to Origen, should be the goal of one's life.[6]

The treatise appears to have been written in haste, in order to provide assurance to Ambrose and Protoctetus who were in danger of suffering martyrdom. It is a work written from the heart, an impassioned plea to his friends to remain steadfast in their hour of trial and not to apostalize, to seek a way out of martyrdom by denying Christ. As a result, the work is not well organized, it is often wordy and repetitive. Unlike most of Origen's works, there is very little allegory in the treatise and it is lacking in philosophical interpretation. It is a sincere and moving document revealing Origen as a humble, loyal servant of the Church with an ardent desire for martyrdom not shared by most. The work is comprised of 51 sections and can be divided into seven major parts: (1) sections 1–5, (2) sections 6–10, (3) 11–21, (4) 22–27, (5) 28–44, (6) 45–46, (7) 47–50.

Origen begins the treatise by quoting Isaias 28:9–11. He reminds his friends that in accordance with the Isaian principle, they are no longer babes in Christ, and therefore they must endure steadfastly, for their suffering will be rewarded with eternal blessedness, shortly. By martyrdom, the Christian shows his perfect love for God and desire to be united with Him. It is only the individual who departs from life with the single purpose of entering the Kingdom of Heaven that will find eternal happiness.

In the second part (6–10), Origen strongly warns against idolatry and apostasy. The most serious sin, he claims, is to deny God and to venerate false gods or idols. God is a jealous God, and like the bridegroom who is concerned that his bride be faithful to him, He will not allow an individual to stray, but attempts to save all souls from idolatry. However, anyone who is unfaithful and commits the crime of idolatry and enters into union with the false gods will be severed from God like a cutting by a sharp sword and will endure severe punishment after death

Part three (11–21) once again exhorts the Christians to endure their trials with perseverance and to bear the cross with Christ unflinchingly. This is the pledge or covenant that an individual makes upon becoming a Christian, and it must not be broken. The reward of the martyr's endurance and self denial will be far greater than any earthly possession that is left behind. Origen reminds the addressees that the whole world, men as well as angelic and evil powers, will be watching their struggle to uphold the Christian religion. Their martyrdom will be hailed by the angels; their apostasy will delight the demons. Therefore, they must guard against being included among the fallen angels. To encourage the martyrs, Origen in the fourth part (22–27), cites excerpts from the Second Book of Maccabees of what he considered brilliant examples of courageous endurance: the old Eleazar (II. Macc. 6:19–31) and the seven brothers and their brave mother (II. Macc. 7).

The fifth part (28–44) deals with the necessity and value of martyrdom. As the supreme expression of gratitude to God, martyrdom is an obligation of all Christians. Moreover, it is only through martyrdom that post-baptismal sins are forgiven. The martyr's sacrifice expiates not only his sins, but also the sins of those who pray to him. In addition, a martyr is able to bring blessings on his children who might be left behind. Origen believed that martyrs are the elect of God, and enjoy a special and greater blessedness. They sit by God's side in communion with Him, sharing His authority and serve as His fellow-judges. Martyrs will share in Christ's consolation in proportion to the sufferings that they share with Him. On the other hand, those who deny God and His Son, either by idolatry or apostasy, will in turn be denied by Them. Thus, Christians are urged to be ready for martyrdom at all times.

Part six (45–46) is a digression from the exhortation and deals with the popular liberal views concerning idolatry. Origen refutes the notion held by some Christians that if he believed in his heart, it did not matter if he either sacrificed to the pagan idols or invoked God by another name in order to avoid persecution. He claims that anyone who sacrifices to the idols feeds the demons and thus is as responsible as they for the wicked deeds that they commit. Moreover, God should not be invoked by any name except those names used by Moses, the prophets and Christ. It is not sufficient to honor God only with the heart; one must also be ready to confess Him with the mouth if one is to receive salvation.

The last and seventh part (47–50) is a final exhortation to courage in times of danger and duress. Origen concludes the treatise, section 51, by expressing the hope that what he has written might be useful to his friends during their conflict. On the other hand, they may have already reached a greater level of apprehension, and thus his efforts may prove to be simple and unnecessary.

Although written primarily for Ambrose and Protoctetus, the work carried a message for all Christians of the time living under the fear of persecution. Besides the encouragement that it offers, it also serves to clarify certain issues and opinions regarding idolatry and apostasy. The document is significant for several reasons. It is important for understanding, (1) Origen's religious loyalty and exalted views of martyrdom, (2) the spirit and concerns of the third century Church and, (3) it provides a historical source for the persecution of Maximinus Thrax (A.D. 235–237).

III. On Prayer

The treatise *On Prayer* is considered one of Origen's best and most uncomplicated works. Like the *Exhortation to Martyrdom*, it is relatively free of his usual allegorical and exegetical interpretations. Westcoff states that "no writing of Origen is more free from his characteristic faults, or more full of beautiful thoughts."[7] The work is in itself a beautiful prayer containing many spiritually suggestive and inspiring thoughts. More than any other of his works, it shows Origen's humble faith and deep devotion to God. It reveals him as a man of prayer. Similar to the *Exhortation*, it was written for a particular purpose; it is a reply to specific questions on prayer posed to him by his friend and patron Ambrose and a certain Tatiana. However, Origen went beyond just answering the concerns of the addressees. Through a carefully selected series of Scriptural quotations, he established a basic guide to the practice of prayer. The treatise gives instruction on how to pray, the proper disposition of the mind in preparation for prayer, the correct posture, place and time for prayer, the various types of prayer, and a detailed commentary on the Lord's Prayer. The work consists of five main sections which include: (1) chapters 1–2 introduction, (2) chapters 3–17 a general discussion of prayer. (3) chapters 18–30 a commentary on the Lord's Prayer, (4) chapters 31–33 supplementary notes to the general discussion on prayer, and (5) chapter 34 conclusion.[8]

The introduction contains a general statement on man's inability to comprehend the divine truths. It is impossible for human nature alone to acquire the wisdom needed to understand the higher truths of nature and those beyond nature. This is only possible by the grace of God ministered by Christ and the Holy Spirit through prayer. Man does not even know how to pray or what to pray about. This information is derived from the Holy Scriptures.

In part two, chapters 3–17, Origen begins by tracing the Scriptural meaning and usage of the word prayer. Generally, the word is used of someone who vows to do a certain thing, if he obtains from God that which he requested. He then proceeds to answer the following questions concerning prayer raised by Ambrose: (1) If God foresees the future and knows man's needs, and (2) if all things are predetermined by Him and cannot be changed, then why is prayer necessary? Origen states that although God foresees and predetermines, He does not interfere with the exercise of man's free will nor absolve him of the responsibility for his actions.[9] Moreover, His foreknowledge takes into consideration man's prayer or his failure to pray. To claim that prayer is unnecessary is either to deny the existence of God, or to accept the name of God but to deny Providence.

The advantages of prayer are many. It establishes an active communion with the Divine and a participation in the Divine life, and it permits the soul to rise above the material things and to contemplate the divine beauty and its mysteries. Frequent communication with God helps to purify the soul from sin; to fortify it against temptation and evil spirits. The best example of this is Christ and the angels. Christ prays for those who pray and intercedes for them with the Father; the angels also, and the souls of the saints carry man's petition to God. Thus, one ought to engage in actual prayer at least three times a day. In fact, Origen claims, man's whole life should be a continuous prayer. By this he means that man's actions, his way of life, should be a part of his prayers; prayers and deeds or actions together should form the whole of man's life. The prayers of one who prays continuously will always be heard. Prayer is a must for all. Even Christ obtains His request only through prayer. How then can man neglect to pray. Origen cites examples from the Scriptures of answered prayers: Daniel in the lion's den (Dan. 6:16, 22); Jonah in the belly of the whale (Jonah: 1:17ff.); Ananias, Azarias and Misael, who with their prayers prevented "the flame of fire" from exerting its power (Dan. 3:24, 49–50) and others. Similar prayers continue to be answered, as witnessed by the many Christians who have experienced deliverance from more harmful beasts and harsher trials. However, man's petition to or communication with God should not be about small and material things but for the supernatural treasures, the great and heavenly things. In asking for the spiritual benefits, the small and earthly things will be supplied in accordance with each individuals needs.

Quoting St. Paul's 1 Tim. 2:1, Origen states that there are four varieties of prayer: petition, intercession, praise and thanksgiving. All of these types of prayer except praise may be offered to God, Christ and to the saints. However, praise, the highest form of worship offered about matters of importance, which includes divine adoration, should be directed only to God the Father. The reason for this, he claims, is that one should never praise a generated being, not even Christ. Moreover, Christ Himself prayed to the Father and taught man also to pray to Him. Thus, invocation may be made of the Son and of the saints, but prayer in the sense of praise or adoration must be directed to the Father through the Son who has been appointed by the Father as the high priest and mediator of all prayers. Without Christ, no prayer can be offered to the Father. By limiting prayer, defined by him as praise to God alone, it appears that Origen was attempting to establish a uniformity in the practice of prayer in the early Church. He asks, "Are we not divided if some pray to the Father, others to the Son?" Therefore, one can fall into a sin of ignorance because of lack of inquiry and examination. However, in subsequent years, this view caused him to come under suspicion of heresy by the Church.

Part three, chapters 18–30, is devoted to an exposition of the Lord's Prayer. Origen begins by comparing the texts of the prayer as found in the Gospel of Luke and Matthew, and claims that the prayers are basically different but have some common parts. His exposition is based primarily on the version found in St. Matthew with occasional references to the St. Luke version. Then, having carefully examined the Scriptures for this point, he notes that the use of the term Father for God in prayer is particular to Christians, and it affirms their relationship to God as children of God. However, this relationship is not merely one of kinship. It involves a state of continuous prayers, of conforming to the divine image through good deeds and actions. Only those individuals who have integrated their devotional and practical lives can truly be called children of God and have the right to recite the prayer.

The whole of the Prayer is interpreted as a petition of the soul for aid in its advancement toward perfection. The "daily bread" requested in the Prayer is the divine nourishment, the divine guidance and illumination which provides health, strength and vigour to the soul to help it to avoid temptation, to keep the mind keen and alert to the good and to continue in its good works and its advancement towards the Divine. In his discussion of the petition "forgive us our debts as we also forgive our debtors", Origen states that man not only owes debts to others with respect to kind treatment and a charitable disposition, but he also owes a debt to himself not to waste his body's powers in pleasure. Above all, man, as the work and image of God, is under a debt to maintain a certain disposition towards Him, that is to love God with his whole heart, strength and mind.

In the closing chapters, 31–33, Origen discusses the proper spirit, place and posture of prayer and the four parts of which each prayer should consist. Prayer, he claims, in order to be effective, must be done after the soul has prepared itself by becoming detached from earthly concerns. The individual should put aside all malice towards anyone that has wronged him, turn away from all disturbing thoughts and impressions and concentrate solely on God's greatness. It is preferred that an individual pray standing upright with outstretched hands and uplifted eyes, facing the East from where the sun rises. This symbolizes the soul looking towards the rising of the true light. The most suitable place to pray is in a church, but a quiet place that offers the minimum of distraction and has not been desecrated is also acceptable. Origen claims that prayer should consist of the following four parts: (1) the glorification of God through Christ in the Holy Spirit; (2) thanksgiving, both general and specific; (3) confession of sin and petition for deliverance from the habit of sin and for forgiveness of past sins; (4) petition for great and heavenly things both for oneself, one's family, friends and for all in general. Finally, prayer should end as it began, by glorifying God through Christ in the Holy Spirit.

The treatise concludes in chapter 34 with the request that the addressees read the work with indulgence until such time when Origin could treat the subjects mentioned in the treatise "with greater breadth and elevation and clarity". There is no evidence that Origen wrote a follow-up to the treatise. However, the ideas on prayer presented in this work had a major effect on the development and understanding of prayer both in the Eastern monastic rules and in the Eastern Church in general.

IV. On The Passover

This work is an allegorical or spiritual interpretation of the twelfth chapter of Exodus. Similar to his homilies and other works on the Scriptures,[10] Origen explains the Exodus passage symbolically to describe the individual Christian's spiritual edification, his continuous progress from the earthly to the spiritual life. This he accomplishes through the etymology of "pascha", the feast's name. The word, originally "phas" is a Hebrew word that was Hellenized to pascha and means "passage". Origen contends that the meaning "suffering", or the passion of Christ applied to the word by most Christians is incorrect.

Origen believed that Scripture has both a literal and a spiritual meaning.[11] Thus, Pascha or the Passover is more than a historical account of an event experienced by the Israelites. The Passover correctly understood as "passage" also symbolizes the continuous passage, the various levels of edification of the individual Christian soul as it passes or travels from the life of the passions to one of virtuous living. This passage or development is a gradual process, a passing of the soul through various stages. Progress at each stage of development is facilitated by God's grace through Christ who is apprehended differently by each individual according to their need, ability and spiritual progress.

The treatise on the Passover is another example of Origen's allegorical expertise and his deep spiritual understanding of the Scriptures which was made known to him through the careful and exact analysis of the grammatical and historical detail of each Scriptural passage.

V. Letters

Origen's first surviving letter is in answer to one from Julius Africanus, an eminent Christian scholar and writer of Nicopolis in Palestine.[12] In a public debate with a certain Agnomon, at which Julius had been present, Origen made reference to doctrinal proofs found in the History of Susanna of the Book of Daniel. In a short, concise letter, Julius challenged Origen's use of the text as authentic and attempted to prove it false through a critical textual analysis of the work. His objections are based principally on the fact that (1) the text of Susanna is found only in the Septuagint—the Greek version of the Hebrew Old Testament, and not in the Hebrew Scriptures; (2) the style and language is different from the rest of Daniel; and (3) most important of all, the paronomasias or play on words between "prinos" (holm-tree) and "prisis" (saw asunder), "schinos" (mastich-tree) and "schisis" (rend) indicate that this addition to the Book of Daniel could not have been composed in Hebrew. The words "holm-tree" and "saw asunder", and "mastich-tree" and "rend" sound alike in Greek, but they are very different in Hebrew. Thus, Africanus concludes that the work was spurious, a modern forgery written originally in Greek, an addition to the original Book of Daniel and thus could not be considered as canonical, not officially approved or accepted as authoritative.

Origen's prejudicial view of the Septuagint would not permit him to be convinced by Africanus' arguments. In a lengthy, drawn-out letter he attempted to rebuke Africanus' cogent statements. However, he fails to present an adequate explanation. His defense is very weak, completely lacking in historical criticism. He states that the text is lacking from the Hebrew Bible because it was purposely omitted by the Jews in order to save the reputation of their elders. The puns or play on words, he contended, were probably introduced by the translator. However, this does not prove that a Hebrew original did not exist. Origen regarded the Septuagint as an independent, divinely inspired authority. As such, it was not possible that it could be in error. He reminds Africanus that the books of the Old Testament had been established and officially recognized by the Church, and states that it would be prudent to remember the words found in Proverbs: "Thou shalt not remove the ancient landmarks which thy fathers have established." (Prov. XXII. 28)

Origen's answer to Africanus indicates his deficiency in handling, critically, historical questions pertaining to established Church traditions. His aim was always to uphold the traditions of the Church, and this sometimes hampered his judgement. In contrast to Origen, Africanus was able, in presenting his argument, to divorce himself completely from his beliefs and not to be biased by his faith.

The letter to his former pupil Gregory is contemporary to Africanus. It is an especially brief letter and thus assumed by some scholars to be a fragment of the original. The letter is part of the selected works in the *Philocalia* and constitutes the whole of chapter three.

Gregory was a pupil of Origen's in his school in Caesarea for five to eight years between the years A,D. 233 and 239–240.[13] At the end of his studies with Origen, he delivered in his honor a panegyric or farewell address.[14] It is not certain whether Origen's letter to Gregory was composed before or after Gregory's address to him. Most scholars, however, seem to favor the view that it was written prior to Gregory's address. When Origen composed the letter, Gregory had not as yet decided what career or profession to pursue—law or philosophy. He advises Gregory to devote himself to the study of theology and the Scriptures, but not to give up the study of philosophy completely. Philosophy should be used as preparation for the study of theology and to explain the sacred Scriptures. Origen did not believe that philosophy was a guide to the understanding of the Scriptures, but only an aid, a preparatory subject. He illustrates the relationship of philosophy and all secular learning to Christianity as being similar to the spoiling of the Egyptians in the Book of Exodus. Just as the Jews took the vessels of gold and silver from the Egyptians and made the Holy of Holies and other things which pertained to the service of God, so should the Christians extract from the treasures of the mind of the Greeks those things that can be used in the preparation for Christianity. However, warns Origen, there is a danger in this procedure. The study of philosophy and other secular learning can lead to heretical ideas. Thus, he admonishes Gregory to apply himself diligently to the study of the Scriptures, and to pray for divine guidance in understanding their hidden meanings in order not to produce rash or false notions about them.

It should be noted that upon completing his studies under Origen's tutelage, Gregory returned to his homeland, Pontus in Asia Minor, and became a pioneer missionary. He subsequently was ordained the first bishop of the province. His devotion to the service of God earned him the name "Wonder Worker" or "Thaumaturgus" and great popularity as a saint after his death. His popular reputation made him the subject of much legendary lore. Tales of exorcisms and marvels wrought by his hand were told about him long after he was gone.

V. Philocalia

According to the preface of the text, the work was compiled by Basil the Great and Gregory Nazianzus. The latter sent it to Bishop Theodore of Tyana with an introductory letter stating that the volume was sent as a memorial from him and Basil containing selected passages from the various works of Origen considered beneficial to scholars, with the hope that the Bishop would give them some proof of its usefulness.

The text is valuable for preserving passages of Origen's works that are either no longer extant or are found only in a Latin translation by Rufinus. It consists of twenty-seven chapters. Of these, the first part of chapter one and chapter twenty-one contain book I. 1 and IV. 1–3, respectively of the *First Principles*. These selection form the larger portion of the extant Greek fragments of the text, and make it possible to ascertain, especially on controversial, or what the Church considered heretical issues, Origen's real views. About a fifth of the text, the last portion of chapter one and chapters fifteen through twenty and twenty-two, contain selections of varying lengths from books I.–VII. of the *Against Celsus*. As mentioned above, chapter thirteen contains Origen's letter to Gregory. The remaining chapters are devoted to fragments from the commentaries and homilies. Included among Origen's extracts is a fragment of Methodius' *Dialogue on Free Will* and a short one from Clement's book ten of the Recognitions. It is not clear why these two fragments were included by the compilers of the anthology. They either incorectly identified them as works of Origen, or included them as supportive statements to Origen's arguments.

A comparison of the Greek fragments of the homilies and commentaries found in the *Philocalia* with Rufinus' versions indicates the extent to which Rufinus either modified, abbreviated or expanded the various works in his translation. In many instances' Rufinus' Latin translations have very little, if any, similarity to the corresponding Greek fragments in the *Philocalia*.

The passages included in the work deal primarily with Scripture, its value and divine authority. In general, the fragments from the *First Principles* are concerned with the inspiration of divine Scripture and how it should be read and understood. Those from the *Against Celsus* are a reply to the Greek philosophers who deny the significance and authority of the Scriptures; and those from the homilies and commentaries discuss the special character of Scripture and the problems encountered in reading and understanding it. Many of the passages illustrate Origen's use of allegorizing Scriptural passages to discover the deeper, philosophical meanings.

The *Philocalia* is of great significance, not only for the excellent passages which are preserved within it, but it also gives an indication of what the Fathers of the Church during the fourth century considered to be important and distinctive thoughts of Origen.

7

Works on the Scriptures

Origen's principal works and the great bulk of his literary output is devoted to the Scriptures. This material comprises more than three quarters of his writings and includes two main types of works, his great critical work, the *Hexapla*, and his exegetical writings. The latter are found in three different literary forms: commentaries, homilies and scholia, by means of which he interpreted almost every book in the Old and New Testament.

I. Hexapla

The *Hexapla* is considered one of Origen's most important scriptural works. It is a sixfold edition of the Old Testament and is considered to be the first attempt in the field of biblical criticism. The work is believed to have taken twenty-eight years to complete. It was begun in Alexandria sometime before A.D. 215 and was completed sometime between A.D. 240 and 245 in Caesarea. The purpose of the study was to provide the Church with the true text of the Old Testament in Greek.

The first Greek translation of the Hebrew Old Testament is believed to have been done sometime about the middle of the third century B.C. at Alexandria. It was written in "koine" Greek, the non-classical, everyday Greek language which had been made popular by the conquest of Alexander the Great. The translation came to be called the Septuagint and carried the identifying symbol of the Roman numeral seventy, LXX. It was so called because, according to Alexandrian tradition, the translation was produced by seventy or seventy-two Jewish elders or scholars. The Septuagint was highly revered as divinely inspired by all Greek-speaking Jews of the Hellenistic world. It was also adopted and sanctioned by the Christian Church as a product of divine authority and inspiration. Moreover, the Christians used the text in their Gentile mission and in controversy with Jewish opponents. In particular, they made great use of the Messianic prophesies found in the Old Testament. The use of the Septuagint by the Christians, as well as the development of rabbinic Judaism in the second century A.D. with its adherence to the more literal sense of the Old Testament, caused the Jews to be increasingly dissatisfied with the Septuagint and they questioned its authenticity. As a result, three new Greek translations of the Old Testament appeared in the second century, the versions of Aquila, Theodotian and Symmachus.

Aquila, a contemporary with Hadrian, from Pontus, was a Christian convert to Judaism. He prepared his translation in A.D. 128–129. The purpose of his work was to prepare an extremely literal translation from the Hebrew into Greek and thus to do away with the interpretations in the Septuagint which seemed to support the views of the Christian Church. Sometime later in the same century, about A.D. 180–186 during the reign of Commodus, Theodotion from Ephesus, also a convert to Judaism, produced a translation of the Septuagint which was intended to be a provision of it, a corrected, amended version. This version is basically a transliteration of the Hebrew text. At the end of the same century, during the reign of Septimus Severus (A.D. 193–211), Symmachus, a member of the Judaic-Christian Ebionite sect, provided the sect with an Old Testament version of its own. His aim was not to render a literal translation, but to give the general sense of the Hebrew text and to interpret the text to support his heresy.[1] In addition, through the years, there was a tendency on the part of the copyists of the Septuagint to make their own alterations or improvements arbitrarily.

These factors, the increasing controversies between Jews and Christians concerning the authenticity and validity of the

Septuagint, and the proliferation and arbitrary altering of the Septuagint text, led Origen to undertake the Herculean task of rectifying the text, critically restoring it to its original purity by providing a text more reliable than any existing at the time, and showing its relationship to the Hebrew original. To prepare himself for the task, he studied the Hebrew language. Aided by his benefactor Ambrose, he traveled throughout the East collecting all existing Greek versions of the Old Testament, which he collated and analyzed along with the Hebrew text. The work took the form of six parallel columns, hence the name *Hexapla*, i.e., the six-fold or six column Bible. Each page showed the total of the manuscripts to be analyzed, the Hebrew and the four Greek versions in common use at the time, those of Aquila, Symmachus, Theodotion and the Septuagint. In the first column he placed the Hebrew text, in the second the same text transliterated in Greek letters in order to show the pronunciation, in the third column the version of Aquila, in the next that of Symmachus, in the fifth the Septuagint and in the sixth column the version of Theodotion. The entire Old Testament was treated in this way. When he analyzed the Psalms, he added three more anonymous versions, thus increasing the columns to a total of nine and changing the *Hexapla* to an *Enneapla*, i.e., ninefold. It is not certain why or where the anonymous versions were produced. All that is known is that one was found in Nicopolis near Actium and one in Jericho.[2]

Origen's critical work is contained primarily in the fifth column of the work, the text of the Septuagint, which he marked with certain critical signs to show its relationship to the Hebrew original. The obelus ($\div$) and the asterisk (*) were used to indicate redundancies, omissions and transpositions of the original. The obelus was used to indicate all additions, words and paragraphs found in the Septuagint but missing in the Hebrew text. A wrong translation found in the Septuagint was corrected and also indicated by an obelus. What was missing from the Septuagint but found in the Hebrew and in one or more of the other Greek texts was marked by an asterisk.[3] The missing words or passages were supplied by Origen primarily from the Theodotion version which was more akin to the Septuagint, as it was a revision of it. An obelus and an asterisk were used together to indicate that the passage or passages were out of order in the Septuagint.

It has been calculated that the whole of the *Hexapla* consisted of nearly fifty volumes, Much too cumbersome for common use and too costly to transcribe. It was placed in the library of Pamphilus in Caesarea, Palestine, at the disposal of scholars. The library was destroyed in the seventh century, along with the *Hexapla*. Today, nothing remains of the work except a few fragments. Although the whole work was never reproduced, some parts of it were. In particular, the fifth column, the Hexaplar text of the Septuagint with all the corrections, was copied many times and widely circulated separately throughout Palestine. In the seventh century, a Syrian translation of it was made which is extant today.

The work is considered the first and one of the best of all early works of biblical criticism, and greatly influenced subsequent studies of textual criticism. Origen was the first major textual critic, and might well be called the father of biblical science. However, he was not a master in the art of higher criticism. Although he sometimes gave an opinion as to what reading was the true one, he made no real attempt to critically determine the correct reading. His primary aim was to note the extent and type of differences found between the Hebrew and Septuagint text. In addition, he did not have a critical or in depth knowledge and understanding of the Hebrew language, and he was hampered by his allegiance to the Septuagint which was considered an inspired unity, a part of the Church's tradition, and thus had to be accepted and defended. This is clearly evident in his *Letter to Africanus*.[4]

II. Commentaries

Origen can be considered not only the first major textual critic, but also the first great Christian interpreter of Scripture.

Others before him, both Christian and Gnostic had engaged in Scriptural interpretation or exegesis, but he was the first to present a scientific interpretation of Scripture, the first to interpret or view each Scriptural passage in relation to the whole.

The commentaries are a blend of grammatical, textual, linguistic, historical expositions and philosophical and theological observations. Origen's lack of knowledge of Hebrew in handling the *Hexapla*, is more than compensated in the commentaries by his thorough, precise verbal and grammatical analysis of the Greek scriptural texts, particularly the New Testament. He believed that Scripture is full of mysteries, every particle has its secret meaning, and the aim of the interpreter is to discover this meaning through very careful and exact analysis of detail (Comm. John XX. 29). Thus, he paid attention to even the minor points of grammar, punctuation and terminology, and took great care to trace each word through every passage in Scripture in which it was used, noting other possible senses and suggesting various etymologies. As a result, the commentaries sometimes are excessively long, repetitive and lack clarity and sequence. Despite these limitations, they are a masterpiece of allegorical interpretation, by means of which Origen finds a spiritual or mystical sense in practically every passage of Scripture, often at the neglect and denial of the literal sense. Although this led him into many errors of interpretation, the commentaries reveal a deep spiritual grasp and penetration of the Scriptures that is not found in many of the later exegetes.

Origen's main purpose in writing the commentaries was to discover and reveal the spiritual sense of Scripture through allegorical exegesis. He believed that the whole of Scripture has three senses—the literal, moral and spiritual, the spiritual alone being of true value;[5] and he would not accept the notion that historical facts are the chief outcome of a Scriptural narrative (Comm. John X. 15–17). Thus, the form that he adopted for this work was to give consecutively first the literal, then the moral and then the spiritual sense of each verse, with the primary interest and emphasis on the spiritual or mystical sense.

According to Eusebius, Origen began his work on the commentaries at the request of his friend and benefactor Ambrose, who provided him with funds for stenographers and copyists (H.E. VI. 23). It is believed that he wrote 291 commentaries on the Old and New Testament. Of these, 275 of the Greek have been lost completely and very little is preserved in Latin. Much of what has survived exists in the catenas, quotations of later ecclesiastical authors and biblical manuscripts. Of the New Testament commentaries, considerable portions of the Commentaries on St. John, St. Matthew and the Epistle to the Romans have survived.

The *Commentary on the Gospel of St. John* is one of Origen's most important commentaries. It is considered his first major exegetical work and the earliest work of Christian exegesis available. However, Origen was not the first to write a commentary on Scripture. There were several older Christian exegetes of whose works only fragments survive. In addition, during the second century, the activity of interpreting the Scriptures was carried on extensively in the Gnostic community. As early as the later part of the second century, about A.D. 160–180, the Valentinian Gnostic Heraclean had written a commentary on the Johannine gospel, and it has been suggested that his work may have suggested the idea to Origen.

Origen's commentary initially comprised more than thirty-two books. Today only nine books are extant, books I, II, VI, X, XIII, XIX, XX, XXVIII, XXXII and small fragments of IV and V. The initial impetus to write the work was to refute the ideas presented in the work on the same gospel of the Gnostic Heraclean. It was undertaken at the request of his friend and mentor Ambrose whom he had converted from Valentinianism, and to whom it is also dedicated. The first four volumes were written in Alexandria sometime between A.D. 226 and 229, the fifth was written during a trip to the East sometime during A.D. 230–231, and the remainder after his arrival at Caesarea. The total work includes a discussion of the Gospel beginning with the prologue through John XIII. 2–33. The remainder of the Gospel was never treated.

110

In general, the Commentary (1) stresses the importance of the spiritual meaning of the Gospels and in particular the Gospel of John, a subject which he first discussed in the fourth book of *First Principles*;[6] and (2) it develops in greater detail Origen's doctrine of the Logos, his person and relationships to God the Father; a subject also introduced in *First Principles* (I. 1–3).

Concerning the Gospels, he states that the Gospels are the "first fruits of the Scriptures," and the gospel of John the first fruits of the four (I.6). The other three gospels speak primarily of Jesus the man, while the Gospel of John, the eternal or spiritual gospel, speaks of the spiritual Christ, the glorified God, the Logos (I.9).

According to Origen, the Logos is the reason or wisdom of God. As such, he dwells with God and has existed with Him from the beginning, i.e., he existed from the beginning as God's wisdom which contained all things in idea before they existed (I. 22). Origen lists and discusses various meanings for the term beginning. The chief one being demiurge, the instrument through which all creation is accomplished. Thus it is logically prior to all other titles attributed to Christ (I. 16–22). The Logos is the Son of God, the first-born of God, incarnated in Christ. He is the invisible image of the invisible Father's power, eternally begotten by the Father. This image comprises the unity both in nature and in substance of the Father and the Son (II. 6).

Having established the divinity and eternal existence of the Son, Origen proceeds to guard against modalism and adoptianism. Modalism maintains that the difference between the Father and the Son is in name only, they are adjectival names used to describe the one divine substance and deny that the Son has a substantial reality of his own. Adoptianism advocates that Christ was only a mere man who because of his extreme goodness was adopted by God as his son at the time of his baptism and was elevated to divine status. To avoid any taint of either thought, he stresses that although the Logos is an image of the Father, he is not so identical with the archetype that he can be said to be as much God as the Father himself. He is not "the God", i.e., God in his own right, but a god. His divinity is not his own, but he possesses it as a gift from God the Father. However, having received it, the Logos is the means by which all other beings receive their divinity (II. 2). Hence, although a hypostasis of the Father and classed with the other created spiritual beings, the Son is superior to them in dignity and transcends them all. He is the first of the divine beings, of higher rank than all the others, for he alone dwells with the Father, knows Him in His entirety and does His will in every detail (X. 35; XXXII. 28). Origen maintains that the Son of God, the Logos, by whom all things were made, exists substantially and essentially according to his own substantial reality, numerically distinct from the Father (VI. 38). Thus, the Logos or Son stands between the uncreated absolutely transcendent God and the created many.

God, claims Origen, is absolute unity and simplicity, beyond all thought and essence (I. 20). As such, He can have no contact with the world of multiplicity. Therefore, an intermediary is needed between God the primal unity and the world of the many, an intermediary that is both one and many. This position is fulfilled by the Son or Logos, who was pre-ordained by the Father to make atonement for the world of creation. Between the Father, who is pure unity and the world, which is pure multiplicity, the Son possesses both aspects at once (I. 23). He is the composite unity of a multiplicity, the wisdom, in accordance with which everything has been created (I. 19). Sharing in the multiplicity of the created beings, the Son is able to adapt himself to their diversity, to each being according to his need and ability to receive him; and thus accomplish his mission. Therefore, he is apprehended differently by each individual, in accordance with their spiritual development.

Origen lists the various titles ascribed to Christ in the scriptures (I. 9), and presents a detailed explanation of these names in the second half of Book I (I. 21–39). These titles are only names indicating the many facets of Christ, the many ways that he adapts himself to the capacities of the individuals with whom he is dealing. Thus Christ is apprehended as a physician by those who are sick, as a shepherd or redeemer to those who need guidance (I. 20). However, as an individual progresses in his spiritual development, he is apprehended under other forms and titles, such as light, truth, righteousness, life and wisdom. He is apprehended as wisdom only by those who, having been illuminated by Christ, have attained a high level of spiritual perfection (I. 20). The Logos is like the steps leading up to the holy of holies in the Temple, to the understanding of the divine mysteries and ultimately to unity with the Divine (XIX. 6).

Origen's concept of the Logos did much to establish an understanding of the Logos both in his creative and redemptive role, and to eliminate any modalistic or adoptionist concepts. His view greatly influenced the later development of the doctrine of the Logos and of the Trinity. The Commentary on John and that on the Gospel of Matthew are especially significant for Origen's method of exegesis of the gospels.

Of the *Commentary on St. Matthew*, which was composed in twenty-five books at Caesarea between A.D. 245 and 246, eight books, ten to seventeen, are preserved in Greek. These deal with Matthew 13:36 to 22:33. A larger portion, which deals with Matthew 16:13 to 27:65 is found in an anonymous Latin translation.

A commentary of fifteen books on the *Epistle to the Romans* was composed sometime during A.D. 243–244. Of these only fragments remain of the Greek. These are part of the papyri which were found in Tura, Egypt, in 1941. In addition, fragments from the first and ninth book are contained in the *Philocalia* and in a bible manuscript. There is also a ten book abridged version of the work in a Latin translation by Rufinus. Rufinus' translation is of no help in reconstructing the original. A comparison of the existing Greek fragments with Rufinus' Latin version indicates that Rufinus took great liberty with his translation.

Of the voluminous Old Testament commentaries composed by Origen, only a part of the *Commentary on the Song of Songs*, books 1–4, is extant in a Latin translation also by Rufinus. According to Eusebius, the original work comprised ten books. The first five were written at Athens about A.D. 240, and the rest sometime afterwards in Caesarea (H.E. VI. 23:2). This work is one of Origen's most significant exegetical works on the purified soul's mystical union with the Logos, the last stage in the soul's mystical journey back to God.[7] St. Jerome considered this commentary Origen's most important exegetical work.

The soul, having arrived at the last stage of the soul's mystical ascent, the state of ecstasy, is ready to unite with the Logos. It has been morally purified and has attained considerable proficiency in discerning and understanding the things of nature and of the divine. The soul thinks only of its love for God, a love that is pure and spiritual, and wishes to unite with Him. It is now ready to fully contemplate the Godhead (Prol.). The soul has reached the level of the intuitive contemplative Knowledge of the Godhead. Origen expresses the relationship between the purified soul and the Logos in terms of a mystical marriage. The soul as the bride, after much searching and longing, finally finds the bridegroom, the Logos, and enters into union with Him. At this stage the soul is inspired and fully illuminated or enlightened by the Logos Himself, and receives from Him directly the meaning and understanding of the divine judgements and mysteries (BK. I.). Nonetheless, even in this stage the soul is not completely secure in its vision or contemplation. It continually progresses towards God and falls or lapses from Him (BK. III.). However, Origen believes that once the soul has arrived at the last stage and has perceived the presence of the Logos, and if it continues to pray to God and to praise Him, it will not fall too far away from God. That is, its fall will not be serious, it will fall only a short distance away from God, a distance that is quickly and easily recovered (BK. III.) Finally, after great perseverance on the part of the soul and after much searching, finding, losing and recovering of the Logos, the soul will finally unite with the Logos in a perfect and lasting union. At that time, the soul will be completely purified and one with God. The purified soul will no longer be conscious of anything besides or other than God. The soul is at peace with itself, completely fulfilled. It is possessed of self-knowledge and is secure in its love of God and its contemplation of Him (BK. III.). Origen prefers to believe that once the soul has attained union with the very essence of the Logos and has become one spirit with Him, it would be bound by the chains of His love that it would not be able ever to move away from Him, that its union with the Logos would be a perfect and lasting one (BK. I.).[8]

Origen was not the first Christian theologian to write a commentary on the *Song of Songs*, but he was the first to interpret the text as depicting both the union of the Church with the Logos, and the individual soul with the Logos. Previous to him, Christian commentators had interpreted this work as depicting only the union of the Church and the Logos, and the Hellenistic Jews had interpreted the *Song* to symbolize the alliance of Yahweh with the congregation of Israel.[9] However, it was Origen's interpretation which had a lasting effect and made a major contribution to the development of spiritual theology. The Commentary is considered the first great work of Christian mysticism and was the inspiration for the subsequent works of later mystics through the Middle Ages.

III. Homilies

The homilies of Origen are basically sermons or lectures on selected chapters or passages of Scripture. They were delivered to congregations, often extemporaneously, mainly at Caesarea after A.D. 244, and recorded by stenographers. Approximately 574 homilies were transcribed. Of these, 388 have disappeared completely; 20 on Jeremias are extant in the Greek original, and the remaining 166 are preserved in Latin transactions.

The primary aim of the lectures was the edification of the faithful, to provide nourishment for the spiritual development of their souls. Unlike the commentaries in which Origen is primarily interested in the spiritual sense of the Scriptures, the homilies provide both the moral and spiritual. As with the commentaries, the texts are allegorically interpreted. These writings form the basis of Origen's theology of the spiritual life, and have had a great influence on later spiritual and mystical theology. Whereas the *Commentary on the Song of Songs* depicts the soul's final stage in its long, difficult journey back to God, the homilies describe the soul's development, the various stages of that journey.

Origen's view of the soul's mystical return to God, its internal spiritual progress, is dealt with extensively in his homilies on *Exodus, Numbers* and the *Song of Songs*. Of particular interest and importance is the twenty-seventh homily on Numbers, in which the author presents the forty-two stages of the soul's ascent from the earthly to the spiritual life. This is set forth through the allegorical interpretation of Israel's exodus from Egypt to the Promised Land.

The starting point of the journey comes when the soul realizes the importance of the spiritual life and acquires self-knowledge and understanding. This is the first and most important step. It is of utmost importance that the soul know and understand what it is and how it is moved, or of what substance it is formed and what are its passions and emotions. Only through self-knowledge will the soul discover what it must and must not do, what to improve and what to preserve. When the soul realizes its divine nature, and understands that the true realities within it, it recognizes that it must take up the struggle against sin and the passions (27:6). The spiritual progress begins when it starts to detach itself from all externals, from the world's confusion and wickedness and from the passions and affections. This leads to a state of apathy, a state of moral freedom and sovereignty (27:9).[10] In this state, the soul is capable of confronting its assailants—the powers of evil (27:9).

The soul's next stage is the acceptance and practice of a life of asceticism. This should initially be done on a moderate scale. As the soul advances in its spiritual ascent, more severe ascetic practices should be followed. These include frequent vigils to weaken the body, severe fasting and continual daily study and

116

meditation of the Scriptures.[11] After passing successfully through these stages, the soul arrives at Beelsephon, translated as watch tower. This means that the soul is now beginning to get a distant view of the splendors that are in store for it. The view increases its hope and strength to continue (27:9).

Following this stage, the soul, once again, passes through a difficult period. According to Origen, the times of progress are always the most dangerous. They are periods of internal conflict for the soul (27:10). In the stages that follow, the soul undergoes great spiritual strife. Its rational and irrational part struggle against each other to gain control.[12] During this period, the soul is aided in its efforts by God through spiritual insight and illumination. These the soul receives by means of constant prayer and reading of the Scriptures. The more conflicts and temptations that the soul meets, and the more it strives to overcome them, the more consolation it receives from God. In other words, the soul's knowledge and insight of God increases. As its knowledge of God increases, so does the soul's love for God and its longing for the sight of the divine and the eternal increases. It is the increasing love and longing that enables the soul to successfully overcome the many trials and temptations with which it is confronted and provides it with the strength and courage to continue the journey. It is necessary for the soul to experience trials and temptations, for only by experiencing and overcoming temptations can the soul attain purification (27:11).[13] As Origen allegorically states in his *Homily on Numbers*, "You (the soul) could not have reached the palm-groves unless you had experienced the harsh trials; you could not have reached the gentle springs without first having to overcome sadness and difficulties" (27:11).

During the period of trials and temptations, the soul begins to encounter the gift of visions. It is a time when it begins to see marked progress in its ascent. It has succeeded in detaching itself considerably from worldly things. However, it is at times still tempted or deceived by material things. Not all visions are beneficial for the soul. Some are temptations, a wicked angel that is transformed into an angel of light to tempt the soul. For this reason, it is important that the soul be continually alert to discern or classify the visions which appear to it. The soul that has realized the point where it can identify clearly the class to which each vision belongs, will prove that it has reached the spiritual level.[14]

When the soul has mastered the art of discernment and has begun to judge all things spiritually, i.e., when it follows the dictates of the spirit and not of the body, it has gained supremacy over the bodily passions. The soul has detached itself from the worldly things that are the causes of sin. It is now capable of receiving divine illumination and a more complete understanding of the mysteries and heavenly visions. Complete alienation from the world and its deceptions permits the soul to enter the world of true reality. The soul now arrives at a stage of blessedness. In this state it receives the complete or perfect vision and understanding of God's works and divine mysteries (27:12): the soul has received true gnosis, it has passed beyond the things of sense to the contemplation of things incorporeal and eternal.

However, although the soul has reached the state or contemplation of incorporeal things, it is still not completely free from the worldly temptations. At several stages in its ascent, the soul is tempted by worldly things and its patience is tried. Even at the fortieth stage, two stages before the final one, when the soul is filled with the divine spirit and attains the intuitive contemplative knowledge of the divine realities, it encounters temptation. The possibility of temptation and the lapse of the soul governs, to a great extent, Origen's discussion of the soul's spiritual ascent. Both in the twenty-seventh *Homily on Numbers* and in the *Homilies on the Song of Songs*, the works that deal primarily with the ascent, there is a great emphasis on the soul's continual progress, the tendency to lapse and the overcoming of the temptation to lapse.[15]

As the soul advances spiritually, the temptations become fewer and the strength and protection to fight them greater. Also, the soul is ready and eager to wage war against the evil powers and rulers of this world. This battle will take place not

118

only within the individual soul, but also in the individual's capacity as a minister of Christ. According to Origen, mere contemplation of God is not the ultimate end of the individual who has reached the spiritual level. Such an individual is required not only to continue his contemplation of God, but also to show others the way to Him by becoming His minister (27:12).

The soul now arrives at the last stages of the contemplative life. It arrives at a state of ecstasy, a state in which the soul has acquired self-knowledge and the understanding of true reality. In this stage, the soul has been completely possessed by the Logos and has been transported completely from the things of sense to the things of the spirit. It has rid itself of the illusion and deceptions of the material world and has come to realize that the only true world is that of the spirit. In this stage there is a complete withdrawal from the things of sense, and an understanding of the things divine (27:12).

Having arrived at the state of ecstasy, the soul is ready to unite with the Logos; it is now ready to fully contemplate the God head, to unite with the Logos. This final stage, the union of the soul with the Logos, is dealt with extensively in the *Commentary on the Song of Songs*.[16]

Origen's ascetic concepts and mystical views of the soul, its spiritual journey back to its divine source, which is the main goal of his thought, influenced the thought of many Christian thinkers, both Eastern and Western. He has been regarded by many as a master of the spiritual life, one who has been a major contributor to the Christian spirituality and piety, and the major force of inspiration to monastics and monasticism in general.

Crouzel asks whether it is possible for someone who possessed such insight of the divine, and who introduced much of the language used by later Christian mystics, not to have also experienced the mystical union.[17] He uses as an example a passage in the *First Homily* on the *Song of Songs* in which Origen describes his own experience in the search for the Logos. Origen states, "God is my witness that I have often perceived the Bridegroom drawing near me and that he was, as much as it is possible, with me; then suddenly he varnished and I could not find what I was seeking" (I. 7). He adds that this experience has occurred on several occasions. Taken in its context, it appears that Origen, in this passage, is describing the difficulty of the spiritual ascent, the finding and losing of the Bridegroom—Logos; and not a personal mystical experience.

It does not appear to be of any great importance whether Origen was, or was not, a practising mystic. What is of great significance is his deep concept and interpretation of the spiritual life, which influenced the thinking of Christian mystics and theologians of later ages.

IV. Scholia

The scholia were primarily brief notes, often grammatical and not necessarily original, on difficult and obscure Scriptural passages. They are similar to the marginal notes found in ancient manuscripts. According to St. Jerome (Letter 33), Origen wrote scolia on Exodus, Leviticus, Isaias, Psalms 1–15, Ecclesiastes and the Gospel of St. John. No collection of them has survived, but fragments are found in the catenas and in the *Philocalia*. However, because none are in existence, it is difficult to determine which are Origen's fragments of the scholia commentaries.

8
Lost Works

From Eusebius it is learned that Origen wrote two other dogmatic works besides the *First Principles*, a treatise on the *Resurrection* in two books, and a ten volume work entitled *Miscellanies* or *Stromata*. Both works are no longer extant except for a few fragments. They were written in Alexandria, the *Resurrection* about A.D. 230 and the *Miscellanies* sometime in A.D. 231 before he left the city, as indicated by Origen in the preface of the volumes.[1]

I. On the Resurrection

Of the many teachings of Origen, two in particular were attacked as early as the end of the third century, the pre-existence of the soul and the nature of the resurrected body. The doctrine of the former, although not completely in Origen's own words, is found in the *First Principles*.[2] His views on the resurrection, since the original discussion on the subject has been lost, can be reconstructed from his *Against Celsus*, the Latin fragments of Rufinus' translation found in the *First Principles*; and from the works of Methodius of Olympus (A.D. 270–312) and St. Jerome (A.D. 345–420) who attacked Origen's attempt to spiritualize the Church's doctrine of the resurrected body as heretical.

According to these sources, Origen believed that at the "apokatastasis",[3] the restoration of all rational beings to their original state of purity and equality, all individuals will be reunited with their bodies. However, he was not in complete agreement with the popular conception of the body which was held within the Church. He could not accept the popular notion that man will be resurrected with the same animal or earthly body which he possessed on earth.[4] The resurrected body will be the same as the earthly body, but with a difference. It will be a spiritual body, of an ethereal quality suitable to its spiritual environment. At the "apokatastasis", the soul will become pure spirit. However, wherever the soul is it has to have a body suitable for the place where it finds itself. Therefore, the body, which will continue to serve the purified soul, will also be purified and receive a spiritual quality and nature.[5] Although Origen was not in complete agreement with the Church's popular belief of the resurrection, nonetheless, he was determined to defend it against pagan criticism.[6] To do so, he attempted to present an explanation of the Christian doctrine which would be intelligible to his pagan contemporaries, and one that would also be fundamentally true to the Christian tradition, as he understood it.

The explanation he advanced started with the basic presupposition that the individual soul of man is permanently enveloped or clothed with a body. The material substratum of the soul's body, as with the bodies of all rational beings, is of such a nature that it can undergo every type of transformation.[7] It changes in form and texture in accordance with the soul's moral development and perfection; it can change from a subtle and ethereal nature in its pure state, to one of a coarser and more solid state. However, as the soul is purified, the soul's body is also purified and returns to its original subtle, ethereal and invisible nature.[8] Furthermore, Origen maintains that each body possesses a distinctive or characteristic form or "eidos". It is this characteristic form which gives to the individual body its distinctive characteristics, its individual character. Unlike the material substance of the body which is in a state of constant flux, the form or "eidos" of the body always remains unchanged.[9] To further explain the individual form of the body, Origen describes it as a "logos spermatos" or "spermatikos", a Stoic concept which he adopted and modified.[10]

122

The Stoics held that the "logoi spermatikoi" were active material forms, principles of energy through whose power or activity all individual things came into being. They were considered by the Stoics as seed powers, which organized and formed each individual thing and maintained its identity, and accounted for the continuity of the individual species.[11] In man, these generative principles were the cause of reproduction, were transmitted from parent to child and were responsible for the individual differences or characteristics both of the body and of the soul.[12] Origen agrees with the Stoics that the form of the body, the "logos spermatikos", is the seed power or energy of the body which gives to the body its individual characteristics and maintains its identity in the flux of everchanging matter.[13] He also maintains that the logos is transmitted from parent to child during procreation and that it is the cause of the body's individual characteristics.[14] However, Origen does not agree with the Stoic notion that the logos is also the cause of the soul's development and character. To do so would be to limit and endanger the free-will of the individual and thus remove the burden of moral actions and responsibilities from the individual. Therefore, he maintains that the spiritual development and character of the soul are completely determined by the free-will of the individual.[15]

Origen claims that it is the "logos spermatikos" inherent in each body that will resuscitate the body at the time of the resurrection, although the body will be of a different texture. Adopting the words of St. Paul (I. Cor. XV. 36–44), Origen compares the resurrection to the growth of a grain of wheat which is buried in the earth, survives death and decomposition and is restored and refashioned as a stalk of wheat. In a similar way, the logos of the body will restore and refashion the body in its original form but the body will be of a nature suitable to its new environment. Thus, the resurrected body will have the same individuality as the animal body of its earthly existence but its texture will be different from that of the earthly body. It will be of a subtle, ethereal and invisible nature, suited to the conditions of the heavenly realm in which it is to dwell.[16]

The Church, in the tenth anathema of the council of Constantinople in 543, accused Origen of maintaining that the bodies of individuals will rise spherical at the resurrection. However, this idea appears to be a much later development of Origen's followers. There is no evidence of it either in Origen's extant material, in the translation of Rufinus or the works of Methodius or Jerome whose main concern was to emphasize the heretical aspects of his doctrines.

II. Miscellanies

It is not possible to determine from the title, *Miscellanies* or *Stromata*, the type of material or subject discussed in the work. According to Clement of Alexandria whose work by the same title is still extant, the title represents a work of a variety of subjects, a patchwork of subjects found in different forms and in no particular order.[17] According to St. Jerome, Origen imitated his predecessor, Clement, and wrote ten books of *Miscellanies*. In this work, he compared Christian teachings with those held by ancient philosophers such as Plato, Aristotle, Numenius and Cornutus, and confirmed the Christian dogmas by quotations from these philosophers (*Letter* 70:4).

Of the work itself, only three fragments remain in a Latin translation, and give insufficient indication of their contents. However, from St. Jerome's statement and the little material available, it appears that Origen's *Miscellanies*, similar to that of Clement, contain discussions of various subjects, in which Scriptural views are juxtaposed, compared, and many spiritual or allegorical interpretations of the Scriptures justified by means of Greek philosophy.

9

Conclusion

I. Origen's Contribution

Origen faced continuous controversy for many of his views both in his lifetime and after his death. Even today, there does not exist, nor does it appear that there will be for a long time, any universal agreement concerning the basic nature of his works. Scholars continue to be sharply divided in their understanding and interpretation of him.[1] The main difficulty stems from an attempt by some scholars and theologians to understand him either as a speculative theologian, or a philosopher, or a humanist, and often to judge his thought in terms of the Nicene Creed established in A.D. 325 or the even later Chalcedonian Symbol of A.D. 451. However, Origen cannot be evaluated by these standards.

In analyzing and evaluating Origen's works, it must be remembered that he was a product of his age and environment. He lived at a time of grave transition and unrest, and was a product of the speculative philosophical environment of third century Alexandria. He wrote at a time when the Church was in one of the most difficult times in its history, when it was in the throes of defining its doctrines. During this time, many views were being discussed concerning God, the Trinity, the world and man, his nature and destiny, but the Church had not yet given formal expression to these matters. No council had yet been convened to make decisions and to establish the doctrines of the Church on these issues. It was Origen's intent to present possible answers, principles and predominating ideas and tendencies, but not to establish definite doctrinal views. He wanted nothing more than to be a devout, loyal, orthodox Christian, and lived his life, personally and professionally, maintaining that goal. His views, no matter how bold were meant as suggestions rather than positive statements. In his explication of the Christian account of God, the world and man, he frequently employed the philosophical concepts of the time to express his Christian thought in an intelligible manner. These concepts he revised and reshaped to agree with his understanding of the Christian beliefs. As a pioneer in his attempt to express and explain the Christian view, he was often too daring and too speculative; however, he claimed no conclusions. His bold speculations, energetic imagination and dauntless use of philosophy in the explication of the Christian beliefs led him, unlike many of his contemporaries, to contemplate a world of great magnitude followed by a succession of world-orders, from the first creation when God created all souls equal and free to the final restoration when, after many trials of suffering and discipline, all souls will return to their original purity and perfection. This view of the world and in particular that of the soul and its destiny was greatly controverted by the Church. However, many of these views were put forward for discussion and investigation, not as established dogma. Moreover, some of the ideas for which he was most severely criticized were not original with him, but go back to his predecessors Philo and Clement of Alexandria. In particular, the theses which were condemned by the Emperor Justinian I and the Second Council of Constantinople in A.D. 553 were primarily the development and the interpretation of his views by Evagrius in the fourth century, and not his own.[2]

Nonetheless, despite the many controversies surrounding his name, he has always been considered one of the greatest theologians of the Church, even in his lifetime, and no one, neither advocate nor adversary, could escape his influence. His contributions are many and include all areas of Christian thought. His influence was especially strong in the areas of textual criticism, exegesis of the Scriptures and religious philosophy. He, more than anyone of his time, was influential in

126

establishing and defining the Church's doctrines and the thought of the early Church in general. His textual and critical studies of the Old and New Testament, the *Hexapla*, and commentaries in which he attempted to give the three meanings of each Scriptural verse—the literal, the moral and the spiritual, helped to establish the scientific study and interpretation of the Scriptures. His use of allegory to determine the spiritual and mystical sense of Scripture did much to preserve the Scriptures for the Church, and to establish an understanding of the relationship between the Old and New Testament. Much of the Old Testament in its purely literal interpretation was difficult, if not impossible, to vindicate as Christian literature, and the literal exegeses of either Testament could not be defended against the criticism of the educated pagans. Origen was not the first Christian theologian to employ allegory in the explication of the Scriptures. The method had been adopted in general by the Alexandrian Christian thinkers. However, Origen was the first to formulate it into a system. The scientific method of allegorical interpretation which he established influenced the interpretation of Scripture both in the East and in the West. In addition, the use of allegory made it possible for Origen to show the compatibility of the philosophical culture of the time with the Gospel, within the confines of the Christian tradition and thus, as Harnack states, contributing more than anyone else to the conversion of the ancient world to Christianity.[3]

In the area of religious philosophy, Origen was the first to attempt to present a logical system of the Christian pronouncements of God, the world and man, and to attempt to harmonize theology, cosmology and anthropology. In this attempt, his thought begins with the idea of the supreme reality—God— and ends with the concept of the individual soul's union with Him. Following the Platonic tradition of his time, Origen stresses the absolute immateriality of God. He alone is unbegotten, an absolutely simple and indivisible intellectual nature, permitting no addition of any kind. There is in Him no greater or smaller, no higher or lower. He is absolute unity, the

Monad, the Unit, Mind, the source from which all intellectual nature or mind commences (*Princ.* I. 1:6; *Comm. John* I. 20ff; *Cels.* IV. 14).[4] As mind, God is incorporeal and eternal. Being incorporeal, He is also immutable and impassible, beyond space and time. God transcends all, self-sufficient and self-contained, beyond thought and being. He does not participate in being; He is participated in rather than participates (Cels. VI. 62, 64; VII. 38ff.).

Transcending all, God is also incomprehensible. He is greater than anything man can understand or that can be measured Although transcendent and incomprehensible, He can be known through the Son or Logos and through the beauty of His works, as the sun through it rays. His providence is felt by all, and He manifests Himself through the Son to those whom He considers worthy, in accordance with their ability to perceive Him (*Princ.* I. 1:5–9; *Cels.* VII. 42). Although Origen describes God in abstract terms, He is for him a personal and active being. As spirit, God has within Himself the power to act, He is intelligent, possessed of self-consciousness and will (*Comm. John* XXXII. 28). Although God does not possess the typically human passions and behavior, He is not devoid of all attributes. God, claims Origen, is long-suffering, merciful and has the passion of Love (*Hom. Numbers* XXIII. 2). Thus, God is not Absolute, but Perfect, the perfect being, perfect in all things. Since he is absolutely transcendent, and a complete unity and simplicity, God could not directly create or have contact with a multiple and complex universe. However, His very nature necessitates the existence of the world. Origen believed that God's goodness and omnipotence can never be without an object of their activity. Thus, an intermediary is needed who is midway between God, the uncreated, primal unity and the created world of the many. This intermediary is the Son or Logos, who possesses both aspects at once, the unity of God and the multiplicity of the world (*Comm. John* I. 23: *Cels.* III. 34).

Origen's understanding of the nature of the divine persons and of their interrelationship influenced the development and

128

definition of the Trinitarian and Christological doctrines of later centuries. The terminology that he used to clarify his views was adopted by the Church in its formulation of these doctrines. He taught that the Son or Logos is the first-born of God, the perfect image and wisdom of the Father, the sum-total of His world ideas. As such, the Logos has existed with God from the beginning—as His wisdom, and has no beginning in time. There was never a time when the Logos did not exist. He is eternally generated from the essence of the Father without diminishing the Father's essence. It would be unworthy to think that God ever existed without His wisdom and power, or to assume a beginning of his begetting (*Princ.* I. 2:2–9; *Cels.* VI. 64; *Comm. John* I. 22). Origen compares the generation of the Logos to an act of the will arising from an inner necessity and proceeding from the intellect without being severed, separated or divided from it (*Princ.* I. 2:5–6). This generative act is an outflow or out pouring of the Father's essence (*Comm. John* XIII. 25).

As the invisible image of the invisible Father's power, the Logos is the same in essence as the Father, or "homoousios". Although of the same essence as the Father, the Logos is less than the Father. He is often described as a "second God". He is everything that the Father is but on a different or lower level (*Comm. John* I. 22; *Cels.* V. 39; *Princ.* I. 2:12–13). Thus, the Son or Logos is for Origen a hypostasis of the Father. He exists substantially and essentially according to his own substantial reality, numerically distinct from the Father, the second in number (*Comm. John* VI. 38; X. 21; *Cels.* VIII. 12).

The third stage in the procession of the Godhead is the Holy Spirit, and is considered the first creation of the Father through the Son. It proceeds from the Son as the Son from the Father, and is related to Him as the Son is related to the Father, i.e., inferior to Him. Proceeding from the Son, the Holy Spirit is eternal and incorporeal, and is equal in honor and dignity to the Father and the Son (*Princ.* pref. 4; I. 3:5). Father, Son, and

Holy Spirit form an eternal, divine triad. They are three distinct beings possessing a unity of essence, will and thought (*Cels.* VIII. 12).

Origen's hierarchical order of the Trinity caused him to be accused of subordinationism. However, the subordination which he taught is not of essence but of office and person. His purpose was to establish the Father alone as the source of deity, while justifying the divinity of the Son and the Holy Spirit. For this reason, he first developed the idea of the eternal generation of the Son. This idea and the term "homoousion" which Origen coined to indicate the unity of essence among the three persons of the Trinity were adopted by the Church in its formulation of the Christological and Trinitarian doctrines.

The divine Logos became incarnated in Jesus and assumed a mortal body and a human soul. This resulted in the inseparable union of the soul of Jesus with the Logos. Origen compares this union to that of a mass of iron which has been placed in the fire and ceaselessly flows with a white-hot heat (*Cels.* II. 9; *Princ.* II. 6:6). The union of the divine and human nature formed a single personality—Christ, the God-man (*Princ.* II. 6:3). Origen's views of the person and nature of Christ marked the beginning of a new era in Christological discussions. He was the first to discuss at length the human soul and general humanity of Christ while emphatically maintaining His divinity. He has done more than any other Christian thinker to justify and harmonize the true and perfect humanity of Christ and His true and perfect divinity in one person. He was the first to use the term "God-man" in relation to Christ, a term that became very important in Christian theology, and taught the interchange of attributes. As a result of the union of the two natures in Christ, the attributes of the divine Logos could be given to the human nature of Christ, and His divine nature could be spoken of in human terms (*Princ.* II. 6:3ff). Christ, therefore, was a composite being, at once both totally human and totally divine (*Cels.* I. 66).

According to Origen, the purpose of the Incarnation was the deification of humanity, the union of all individuals with the divine Logos, and represents God's pre-eminent act of redemption of mankind. It was the Logos' greatest attempt to reconcile mankind with God by becoming the example and model for its salvation, the means by which man can return to his spiritual state (*Princ.* IV. 4:4; *Cels.* VI. 68). The various functions and attributes of the incarnated Logos are as a ladder, by which the individual soul advances step by step from his present bodily state to pure spirit. This can be accomplished through the soul's diligent imitation of Christ and through Christ's continual help and guidance at every step of the soul's way back to its spiritual state and ultimate union with God (*Comm. John* II. 8; *Cels.* VII. 32, 43–44; *Princ.* III. 2:2,5).

Origen's doctrine of the soul, its nature and destiny is among his most controverted, and it led to his condemnation by the Church in A.D. 553, at the Second Council of Constantinople. He taught that all souls were created from all eternity as pure spirits, perfect, equal and free. They were participants in the life of the Logos and in perfect communion with God (*Princ.* II. 9:1, 6; IV. 4:9). However, through the exercise of their free-will they fell away from God. Their estrangement from God caused them to lose their initial unity and equality and to take on various types of forms and material textures. The material and form of a soul's body was determined by the degree of its estrangement from the Divine (*Princ.* II. 9:3–4; *Cels.* I. 32). The beings who fell only a short distance from God were clothed in an ethereal body and became the stars, planets and the angels in their various degrees of hierarchy. Those that fell a greater distance were embodied in an earthly human frame, and the spirits who turned completely against God became demonic or evil spirits and are clothed in dark, coarse and unattractive but invisible bodies. Thus, according to Origen, the diversity existing within the created order, the various conditions existing among individuals is a result of the differences among the souls in the degree of their fall. Therefore, an individual's status of birth and the situations that befall him during his lifetime should not be directly attributed to God or to chance, but to the soul's conduct in its pre-existent state (*Princ*. I. 8:1–2, 7:4; II. 2:1, 9:2–3; *Cels*. I. 32).

Simultaneously with the bodies of the fallen beings, God created the material universe to serve as a place for educating and disciplining the souls, a place through which and from which the souls must rise to apprehend and become once again a part of the world of truth and ultimate reality (*Princ*. III. 5:4–5; *Cels*. VII. 50). However, this created world is temporary. All souls will one day be purified and reunited with their Creator. At this time, the visible material universe will cease to exist. Hence, Origen denied the materiality and eternity of hell. The fires of hell are a state of mind. They are the torments of conscience, the soul's remembering of all its evil deeds. It is the punishment the soul must experience because of its unstable and disordered condition, and disciplinary in purpose. Therefore, they are temporary and not eternal (*Princ*. II. 10:4–8; *Cels*. V. 15–16; VI. 25–26).

The doctrine of the "apokatastasis", as Origen calls the restoration of all rational beings to their original state of purity and equality, is unique to his thought and is most typical of his philosophical/theological speculation. It is determined by the principle that the end should resemble the beginning. In accordance with this principle, Origen claims that just as all rational souls came from the divine world, the heavens, so all souls, at an appointed time known only to God, will be completely purified and will voluntarily return to their original state of perfection (*Princ*. I. 6:1; II. 10:8). No rational soul is excluded from this perfect unity in God, no matter how it might have fallen into sin. Created in the image of God, all rational souls share or partake of the divine essence. Even though it has been estranged from God, each rational being always retains within it a spark of the Divine, a germ of goodness, by which it maintains a certain kinship or affinity to God and which in its essence is inaccessible to evil (*Princ*. IV. 4:9–10; *Comm. John* XXXII. 11). At the universal restoration, the purified souls will no longer be conscious of anything besides or other than God,

132

but will think God and see God and hold God and God will be the mode and measure of its every movement. Gods rule will be universal and He will again be all in all (*Princ.* II. 11:7; III. 6:2–3).

The process of purification is realized in each soul gradually and separately at different levels and speeds (*Princ.* III. 6:6). Thus, it may take more than one aeon before the universal restoration is achieved. This restoration, however, should not be regarded as the end of the world, but as a passing phase. Influenced by Plato, Origen taught the endless succession of world orders, one following the other. He claims that this present world which had its beginning at a certain time will also end. It is only one in the succession of corresponding orders. There were worlds before this and there will be worlds after it (*Princ.* III. 5:3).

The creation of another world order is depended on the freedom of the will of the rational beings. Having fallen from God before, it is possible that they might fall again. If so, a new world order will be needed in order for providence to again redeem the fallen beings and bring them back to the Creator (*Princ.* I. 3:8; *Comm. John* X. 42). Thus, the creation of the world becomes a constant, unceasing act.

The eschatological doctrine, or the end of all things, proposed by Origen caused much controversy in the Church. Nonetheless, it had a lasting effect on the early Church Fathers who succeeded him. His doctrine of the individual soul, its nature and various levels of participation in the divine life, served as a foundation for the teaching of the later Fathers on the nature of grace.

Origen was also very influential in the development of the theology of the spiritual life; he is considered the founder of that theology and the forerunner of monasticism. He was the first to describe in careful detail each step of the spiritual journey that the soul follows on its return back to the Divine. His ascetic concepts and mystical views of the soul influenced the thought of many Christian thinkers, both Eastern and Western, who succeeded him. Even those like Bernard of

Clairvaux who condemned him strongly were deeply influenced by him, and the monastic movement, Eastern and Western, through the ages has been indebted to him for inspiration. In fact, his doctrine of the soul in general helped to mold the subsequent Christian concept of man.

Origen views the ascent of the soul as a gradual inner, spiritual development. It is a process by which the soul diligently strives to purify itself, a continual advancement towards the good. First, it purifies itself morally; then, with the grace of God, it develops the sense or knowledge to discern the real from the temporal. As it continues to be illuminated by the Logos, it advances forward until it comes to live purely in the spirit and unites with the Logos. Origen emphasizes that at every step of the way, the soul requires the aid or grace of the Logos. The soul alone does not possess a sufficiently strong will or the ability to obtain union with God through its own insight or self-knowledge, or by merely imitating Christ (*Cels.* VII. 33, 42–44; *Princ.* III. 2:2,5; *On Prayer* XXIX. 19; *Comm. John* II. 8). The way by which the soul ascends progressively to God, whether it is the soul's progression in this life from the things of sense to knowledge of God, or whether it is the soul's journey from this life to the life beyond, Origen finds in the Scriptures, set forth in mystical or symbolic terms.

The soul's mystical return to its Creator, its internal spiritual journey, is described in detail in his homilies on *Exodus*, *Numbers*, and *Homilies* and *Commentary on the Song of Songs*. In particular, the twenty-seventh homily on *Numbers* presents a detailed explanation of the forty-two stages of the soul's ascent from the earthly to the spiritual life. This is accomplished through the allegorical interpretation of Israel's exodus from Egypt to the Promised Land.

The return journey is long and strenuous. Four major stages can be distinguished in this journey of the soul. First and foremost, the soul that has chosen to imitate Christ and attain perfection must acquire self-knowledge and understanding of its true essence. It must understand its passions and emotions; what to do and what to avoid in its progress (*Comm. Song of*

Songs II). The result of self-knowledge is the soul's realization that it must take up the struggle against sin and the passions. The spiritual progress of the soul commences when it begins to detach itself from all externals, from the world's confusion and wickedness and from the passions and affections. This leads the soul to a state of apathy, a state of moral freedom and sovereignty, whereby it can confront and combat its assailants—the powers of evil. In Origen's view, detachment from the world includes the renunciation of marriage. He does not totally reject marriage, but considers the celibate life as superior and recommends it for the individual who wishes to be a true imitator of Christ (*Hom. Numbers* 24:2; *Comm. Song of Songs II*).

Complete detachment from the world can be acquired only by the acceptance and life-long practice of a life of asceticism. The ascetical exercises include frequent vigils to weaken the power of the body, strict fasts, and continual daily study and meditation of the Scriptures (*Homs. Exodus* 12:5; *Jos.* 15:3; *Genesis* 10:3). This is the second major stage in the soul's ascent. Following this stage, the soul once again passes through a different period. It is a period of internal conflict and spiritual strife. The rational and irrational part of the soul struggle against each other for control. This is the first of such conflicts. According to Origen, the times of progress are always the most dangerous for the soul. It is then that the soul encounters the many trials and temptations. However, it is necessary for the soul to experience trials and temptations. Only by experiencing and overcoming temptations can the soul attain purification. The more conflicts and temptations that the soul meets, and the more it strives to overcome them, the more it is aided in its efforts by God, by means of spiritual insight and illumination. That is, the soul's knowledge and insight of God increase. As its insight increases, so does the soul's love for God and its longing for the sight of the divine and eternal. It is this increasing love and longing that enables the soul to successfully overcome the many trials and temptations with which it is confronted, and provides it with the strength and courage to continue the journey (*Hom. Numbers* 27:11; *Comm. Song of Songs* III).

During the period of trials and temptations, the soul receives the gift of visions. The purpose of such visions is to strengthen the soul against future suffering. They are the oases in the desert of suffering and temptation. However, the soul must be careful and continually alert to discern or classify the visions which appear to it. Origen cautions that these visions can and are often used by the devil to tempt the soul. Therefore the soul must learn to discern the thoughts coming from God and those coming from the devil. In this way, it will be able to avoid or overcome those thoughts that will lend it to sin (*Hom. Numbers* 27:11).

When the soul has mastered the art of discernment, it arrives at the next or third stage of development. It has begun to judge all things spiritually, i.e., it has gained supremacy over the bodily passions and now follows only the dictates of the spirit (*Hom. Numbers* 27:12). The soul has detached itself from the worldly things that are the causes of sin and is now capable of receiving a more complete understanding of the mysteries and heavenly visions (*Ibid.*). Having alienated itself from the world and its deceptions, the soul now enters the state of blessedness. In other words, the soul has received true gnosis; it has passed beyond the things of sense to the contemplation of things incorporeal and eternal.

However, even in this state of blessedness, the soul is not totally free from the worldly temptations. At several stages in its ascent, the soul encounters temptations and trials. Most of Origen's discussion of the soul's spiritual ascent is devoted to the soul's continual progress, its lapsing and overcoming of the temptation to lapse. As the soul advances spiritually, as it continues to overcome the temptations that it encounters, the temptations become fewer, and the divine strength and protection to fight them increases. Finally the soul arrives at the last stages of the contemplative life. It arrives at a state of ecstasy, a state of simplification and surrender of the self, an aspiration towards contact which is at once a state of rest and a meditation directed towards perfect conformity or fulfillment. The soul is now ready to unite with the Logos.

The fourth and final major stage in the soul's ascent is its mystical union with the Logos. The soul has been morally purified, has left behind all things of sense, and is inspired and fully illuminated or enlightened by the Logos, from whom it receives directly the meaning and understanding of the divine judgements and mysteries (*Comm. Song of Songs* prol.; I). However, even in this final stage, soul is not secure in its vision or contemplation of God. It is continually perceiving, losing and recovering the Logos (*Hom. Song of Songs* I. 7; *Comm. Song of Songs* III.). Due to its inherent instability, its proneness to lapse, the soul continually vacillates between the visible and the temporal, and the invisible and eternal. Thus, the soul's spiritual progress is one of progression and regression. Origen believes that once the soul has perceived the presence of the Logos, and if it continues to pray to God and to praise Him, even if it lapses, it will not fall too far away from God. Such a soul will not be led far away from the boundary of heaven (*Cels.* VI. 20; *On Prayer* XXV. 2). He prefers to think that once the soul has attained union with the Logos, its love for the Logos would be so binding that it would not be able ever to move away from Him (*Comm. Song of Songs* I.).

According to Origen, the soul's complete union with God cannot be attained in this life, while in a human body. Man's bodily nature is an impediment both to the soul's continuing and uninterrupted contemplation of God and its fitness for union with Him (*Comm. Song of Songs* III; *Princ.* III. 6:3). While in an earthly body, the soul is too weak and unstable to attain complete union with God, even for a rare and brief instant. Clothed in the body, the soul can arrive at the contemplative stage, it can become aware of the Divine, i.e., there is an approach of the Divine to the soul, but it stops short of complete oneness or unification (*Comm. Song of Songs* III; *Hom. Song of Song* I. 7). The soul's complete and lasting union with God can be achieved only after death, and for many souls whose progress is very slow, unity with God may not even be achieved in this age (*Princ.* II. 11:7; III. 6:1–3). Origen's views of the soul's spiritual development, the means by which it gradually and progressively developed spiritually, and its ultimate union with the Logos were adopted by the early monastic writers and have had a great and lasting influence on the development of monastic life.

Origen was denounced and condemed for many of his views during his lifetime and throughout the history of the Church. Yet, despite the numerous attacks and controversies, his influence has been strongly felt and continues to be felt in the life and thought of the Church. His contributions can be found in every area of theology. As Biggs claims, Origen's name has always been a kind of touchstone, and there has never been a truly great man in the Church who has not been influenced by him and who did not love him a little".[5]

Notes and References

Chapter One

[1] Eusebius' *Ecclesiastical History* used in this study is from the Loeb Classical Library, edited and translated by L. Kirsopp and J. E. L. Oulton, *Eusebius: The Ecclesiastical History*. Text and English translation (2 Vols.; London, 1964–65). It is cited in the text as H. E.

[2] P. Koetschau, ed., *Sammlung ausgawahlter Kirchen und dogmengeschichtlicher Quellenschriften*, Heft 9: *Des Gregorios Thaumaturgos Dankrede an Origenes* (Leipzig, 1894).

[3] Unless stated otherwise, the works of Origen used in this study are from the edition of C. H. E. Lommatzsch, *Origen Opera Omnia* (25 Vols.; Berlin: Sumtibus Haude et Spener, 1831–48), and P. Koetschau, *Die Griechischen Christlichen Schriftseller der Ersten Drei Jahrhunderte*, Vol 2, pts. 1–12: *Origenes Werkes* (Leipzig 1891–1955).

[4] The biblical interpretation of Origen is represented by W. Volker, *Das Vollkommenheitsideal des Origenes* (Tubingen, 1931) and H. de Lubac, *Histoire et Espirit: L'Intelligence de l'Ecriture d'anres Origene* (Paris, 1950). The main works treating Origen primarily as a Greek philosopher are E. De Faye, *Origene Sa Vie, Son Oeuvre, Sa Pensee* (3 vols.; Paris, 1925–8) and H. Koch, *Pronoia und Paideusis* (Berlin 1932).

[5] J. Danielow, *Origen*, trans. by W. Mitchell (New York, 1955). pp. X–XIV.

Chapter Two

[1] A large portion of this chapter has been excerpted from Part III of my text, *The Doctrine of the Soul in the Thought of Plotinus and Origen* (New York, 1978).

[2] Cf. *Cratylus* 399 D–E.

[3] *De Anima* I. 2:405b.

[4] Cf. Tertulian, *De Anima* 25, 27, ed. by J. H. Waszink (Amsterdam: J. M. Meulenhoff, 1947).

[5] Origen derives this argument from the Stoic doctrine of theodicy, cf. Plutarch, *Moralia* 1050E, 1065B.

[6] H. A. Wolfson, "Immortality of the Soul and Resurrection in the Philosophy of the Church Fathers," *Harvard Divinity Bulletin*, 22 1956/57), p. 9ff.

[7] Cf. E. R. Dodds, *Proclus, the Elements of Theology* (Oxford, 1963), Appendix II.

[8] Origen's view of the resurrected body is discussed in Chapter 8, pt. I.

[9] Cf. F. Cumont, *After Life in Roman Paganism* (New York, 1959), Chaps. II., III.

[10] B. Darrell Jackson, "Sources of Origen's Doctrine of Freedom," *Church History*, 35 (1966), pp. 13–23.

[11] *Ibid.* p. 15–22.

[12] This statement is also preserved in the *Philocalia* XXI; *On Prayer* VI. 1.

[13] This is also found in Origen's treatise *On Prayer* VI. 2.

[14] See below Chapter 8, pt. I.

[15] This view is found in *Comm. Romans* IV. 16 (Greek fragment); V. 10 *Comm. Matt.* XII. 34; *Comm. Canticles* I.

Chapter Three

[1] Cf. H. Clement *Stromata* V. 8ff., 14.

[2] The spiritual ascent of the soul is discussed below. See Chapter 7, pt. II, III.

Chapter Four

[1] Cf. H. Chadwick, *Origen: Contra Celsum*, English translation (Cambridge, 1965), pp. XXVI. ff.

[2] For a detailed analysis of Celsus' knowledge of and use of the Gospels and other Christian writings, cf. J. Patrick, *The Apology of Origen—In Reply to Celsus* (London, 1892), Chapter III.

[3] Cf. *Stromata* V. 8ff., 14.

[4] Celsus' view that God can be known through synthesis, analysis and analogy is very similar to the view of the Middle Platonist Albinus. Cf. Albinus, *Epitome* 10:21.

[5] Cf. Plato, *Timaeus* 69C,D.

[6] Cf. Plato, *Theaetetus* 176A.

[7] Celsus quotes Herodotus extensively to support his argument for the local religious customs and traditions. See especially Herodotus, Book II.

[8] For a concise listing of the ancient traditions corrupted by the Christians, cf. H. Chadwick, *Origen: Contra Celsum*, English translation (Cambridge, 1965), pp. XX-XXI.

[9] Celsus here quotes from Plato, *Epistle* VII, 341C,D.

[10] Plato, *Phaedrus* 247C.

[11] Homer, *Odyssey* IV. 563–5; Cf. Plato, *Phaedo* 109A, B.

[12] Plato, *Laws* 715E.

[13] Celsus here is not describing the Christian view of humility, but the Christian manner of doing penance.

[14] Matt. XIX. 24; MK. X. 25; LK. XVIII. 25.

[15] Plato, *Laws* 743A.

[16] Plato, *Crito* 49B–E.

[17] Plato, *Republic* 380D; 381B,C; *Phaedrus* 246D.

[18] See above p. 43.

[19] *Ibid*

[20] *Iliad* II. 205.

[21] I Cor. XI. 19.

[22] I Cor. II. 4.

[23] I Cor. I. 18, 24.

[24] Origen's discussion of Jesus' suffering is discussed above on p. 66–67

[25] Origen's doctrine of the resurrected body is discussed below in Chapter 8, pt. I.

[26] *Phaedo* 81D.

[27] Gen. XIX. 10–11.

[28] Matt. XIII. 54; MK. VI. 2; John VII. 15.

[29] I Cor. I. 24.

[30] Origen's doctrine of free-will is discussed above in Chapter 2, pt. V.

[31] Man's relation to God and his spiritual ascent to the Divine is discussed above in Chapter 2, pt. IV, and Chapter 7, pt. III.

[32] I Tim. II. 1–2.

[33] Gen. XVIII. 24–6.

[34] Mt. XXVIII. 19.

Chapter Five

[1] The text is from the edition of J. Scherer, *Sources Chretiennes*, Vol. 67: *Origenes Dialecta cum Heraclides*, Text and French translation (Paris, 1960).

[2] H. Chadwick, *The Library of Christian Classics*, Vol. 2: *Alexandrian Christianity* (Philadelphia, 1954), p. 437.

[3] A. D. Nock, *American Journal of Archaeology*, 55 (1951), pp. 283–284.

[4] Cf. Scherer, *Origenes*, p. 21ff. and Chadwick, *Alexandrian Christianity* p. 432.

[5] Cf. *Against Celsus* I. 45, 55.

[6] Cf. Eusebius, *Ecclesiastical History* VI. 23:4, 33, 37; see above Chapter 1, pt. II., p. 4

[7] Cf. *Against Celsus* II. 9; VI. 47.

[8] Origen also cites Jn. 10:30 in his *Against Celsus* VIII. 12 as proof of the unity between Christ and God. However, in this passage he speaks of "a unity of thought, harmony and identity of will."

[9] This doctrine of prayer is further developed and discussed in Origen's work *On Prayer* XIV-XVI; see below p. 97f. See also Against Celsus V. 4–5 VIII. 13, 26.

[10] A detailed explanation of the relationship between God, the Father, and Christ, the Son, is found above in Chapter 2, pt. II, p. 18f.

[11] Origen derives this interpretation from St. Paul's passages I. Thess. 5:23; Rom. 8:16; I Cor. 2:11.

[12] Eusebius, *Ecclesiastical History* VI. 37.

[13] Genesis 1:26; 2:7.

[14] Cf. Rom. 6:2, 10.

[15] Cf. Ezek. 18:4.

[16] Rev. 9:6.

[17] See especially, *First Principles* II. 3:2; IV. 4:9–10 and *Against Celsus* II. 60; VII. 5.

[18] Chadwick, *Alexandrian Christianity*, p. 436.

Chapter Six

[1] Cf. Eusebius, Ecclesiastical History VI, 2:2–16, where Origen's early youth is described.

[2] The fragments have been edited by O. Gueraud and P. Nautin, *Origene Sur la Paque* (Paris, 1979).

[3] For a recent discussion of the work, see T. Halton, "The New Origen, Peri Pascha", *The Greek Orthodox Theological Review*, 28, 1 (1983), p. 73–80; and J. W. Trigg, *Origen: The Bible and Philosophy in the Third-century Church* (Atlanta, 1983)

[4] The text of the *Philocalia* is from the edition of J. A. Robinson, *The Philocalia of Origen* (Cambridge, 1893).

[5] Psalm 115:3. Origen discusses this in detail in section 28 of the treatise.

[6] See above Chapter 2, pt. IV.

[7] B. F. Westcott, "Origenes", *Dictionary of Christian Biography*, Vol. 4, ed. by W. Smith and H. Wace (New York, 1967) p. 124.

[8] The analysis presented here represents Origen's characteristic views on prayer in general, and his main points of the Lord's Prayer. For a more detailed analysis of Origen's treatment of the Lord's Prayer, cf. H. Chadwick, *The Library of Christian Classics*, Vol. 2: *Alexandrian Christianity* (Philadelphia, 1953) pp. 213–223.

[9] For a discussion of man's free-will see above Chapter 2, pt. V.

[10] See below Chapter 7, especially pt. III.

[11] This is discussed in greater detail in Chapter 7, pts. II and III.

[12] Cf. Eusebius, Eusebius, *Ecclesiastical History* I. 7; VI. 31.

[13] In his farewell address, Gregory states that he had been with Origen for eight years. However, Eusebius claims five years (H. E. VI. 30). It is possible that Eusebius mistakenly wrote E' (five) instead of H' (eight).

[14] See above p. 4.

Chapter Seven

[1] Cf. Eusebius, *Ecclesiastical History* VI. 17, also III. 27.

[2] *Ecclesiastical History* VI. 16; Origen *Letter to Africanus* 4–5; *Comm. Matt.* XV. 14. An excellent study of the development and organization of the *Hexpla* is found in H. Swete, *Introduction to the Old Testament in Greek* (New York, 1968), pp. 59–86.

[3] *Ibid.*

[4] See above Chapter 6, pt. IV.

[5] The three senses of Scripture are discussed above in Chapter 3, pt. II.

[6] See above Chapter 3, pt. II.

[7] The various stages of the soul's mystical ascent are discussed below in the section on the homilies.

[8] Cf. also, *Comm Matt.* XII. 34; *Comm. Romans* IV. 16 (Gk. frag.); V. 10.

[9] Cf. *Canticles Rabbah*. See H. A. Wolfson, *Philo*, Vol. I (Cambridge, Mass., 1947), p. 134.

[10] Origen's terminology of the passionless life is reminiscent of the Stoic doctrine of ethics.

[11] Cf. *Hom. Exodus* 13:5; *Hom. Jos.* 15:3; *Hom. Gen.* 10:3.

[12] Origen's view of the nature of the human soul is discussed above, Chapter 2, pt. IV.

[13] Cf. *Hom. Luc.* 24.

[14] *Hom. Num.* 27:11. The doctrine of the discernment of spirits is an important factor in Origen's spiritual life. It was adopted from him by the early "heremites", or Fathers of the Desert. The doctrine is carefully described in *First Principles* III. 2:1–7.

[15] See especially the *Homily or the Song of Songs* I. 7–8.

16 See above, pt. II.

17 H. Crouzel, *Origene et la Connaissance Mystique* (Paris: Desclee De Brouwer, 1961), p. 529 ff.

Chapter Eight

1 Cf. *Ecclesiastical History* VI. 24:2–3.

2 See above Chapter 2, pt. II.

3 See above Chapter 2, pt. VI.

4 *Cels.* V. 14, 18; *Princ.* III. 6:5ff.

5 *Princ.* I. 8:4; II. 2:2, 3:2, 10:1; III. 6:4–6; *Cels.* VII. 32. and Methodius *On the Resurrection* I. 22:4–5.

6 *Cels.* V. 14–24; VII. 32; VIII. 49: *On Psalm* I. 5.

7 *Princ.* I. 6:4; II. 2:1–2; IV. 3:15; *Cels.* VII. 32.

8 *Princ.* II. 1:4; 2:2; *Cels.* III. 41ff.; IV. 56ff; VI. 77.

9 *On Psalm* I. 5.

10 *Cels.* V. 22ff.; VII. 32; *Princ.* II. 10:3; Jerome *To Pammachius Against John of Jerusalem* 26.

11 F. Copleston, *A History of Philosophy*, Vol I, p. 2: *Greece and Rome*, Image Books (New York, 1946) p. 133.

12 See H. Chadwick, "Origen, Celsus and the Stoa," *Journal of Theological Studies*, 48 (1947), p. 44.

13 *Cels.* V. 18ff.; VII. 32; VIII. 49; *Princ.* II. 10:3

14 *Comm. John* XX. 2–6; *On Psalm* I. 5; *Cels.* V. 22–23.

15 *Comm. Matt.* XIII. 26; also, Chadwick, "Origen, Celsus and the Stoa," p. 44.

16 *Princ.* II. 10:3ff.; III. 6:4–6; *Cels.* III. 41ff.; V. 18–24; *On Psalm* I. 5.

17 Cf. Eusebius *Ecclesiastical History* VI. 13: 4–8.

Chapter Nine

1 For a discussion of the recent arguments concerning Origen, see H. Musurillo, "Recent Revival of Origen Studies," *Theological Studies*, 24 (1963), pp. 250–263.

2 Cf. H. Chadwick, *Early Christian Thought and the Classical Tradition* (New York, 1966), p. 120f.

3 A. Harnack, *History of Dogma*, trans. N. Buchanan 3rd ed. Vol. 2 (New York, 1961), pp. 319, 333.

4 The following abbreviations of Origen's works are used in this chapter: *Princ.* = *First Principles*; *Cels.* = *Against Celsus*. All other abbreviations used are obvious.

5 C. Biggs, *The Christian Platonists of Alexandria* (Oxford, 1913), p. 329.

Selected Bibliography

Primary Sources

BURGES, GEORGE. *The Works of Plato*. English translation. 6 vols. (Bohn's Classical Library). London: Henry G. Bohn, 1849–54.

BUTTERWORTH, G. W. *Origen on First Principles*. English translation. (Harper Torchbooks). New York: Harper and Row Publishers, 1966.

CHADWICK, H. *Origen: Contra Celsum*. English translation. Cambridge: The University Press, 1965.

DODDS, E. R. *Proclus: The Elements of Theology*. Text and English translation. 2nd ed. Oxford: The Clarendon Press, 1963.

GREGG, J. A. F., ed. "The Commentary of Origen Upon the Epistle to the Ephesians." *The Journal of Theological Studies*, 3 (1901–2), p. 233–44, 398–420, 554–576.

GUÉRAUD, O. and NAUTIN, P. *Origène, Sur la Pâque*. Paris: Editions Beauchesne, 1979.

HERMANN, C. F., ed. *Platonis Dialogi*. 6 vols. Leipzig: B. G. Teubneri, 1907–22.

JAY, E. G. *Origen's Treatise on Prayer*. English translation. London: S. P. C. K., 1954.

JENKINS, C., ed. "Origen and I. Corinthians." *The Journal of Theological Studies*, 9 (1907–8), p. 231–47, 353–372, 500–514; and 10 (1908–9), p. 29–51.

KIRSOPP, L. and OULTON, J. E. L. *Eusebius: The Ecclesiastical History*. Text and English translation. 2 vols. (Loeb Classical Library). London: Wm. Heinemann Ltd., 1964–65.

KOETSCHAU, P., ed. *Die Griechischen Christlichen Schriftseller der Ersten Drei Jahrhunderte*. Vol. 2, pts. 1–12: *Origenes Werkes*. Leipzig: J. C. Hinrichs'sche Buchhandlung, 1891–1955.

_____ *Sammlung ausgewahlter Kirchen und dogmengeschichtlicher Quellenschriften*. Heft 9: *Des Gregorios Thaumaturgos Dankrede an Origenes*. Leipzig: J. C. B. Mohr, 1894.

LAWSON, R. P. *Origen: The Song of Songs, Commentary and Homilies*. English translation. Vol. 26 (Ancient Christian Writers). Westminister, (Md.): The Newman Press, 1957.

LOMMATZSCH, C. H. E., ed. *Origen Opera Omnia*. 25 vols. Berlin: Sumtibus Haude et Spener, 1831–48.

MEHAT, A. Sources Chretiennes. Vol. 29: *Origene: Homelies sur les Nombres*. French translation. Paris: Les Editions du Cerf, 1951.

MENZIES, A., ed. *The Ante-Nicene Fathers*. Vols. 2, 4, 6, 10. Michigan: Wm. B. Eerdmons Publ. Co., 1951.

METCALFE, W., ed. *Translations of Christian Literature*. Series I, Greek Texts: *Gregory Thaumaturgus Address to Origen*. New York: The Macmillan Co., 1920.

O'MEARA, J. J. Origen: *Prayer and Exhortation to Martyrdom*. English translation. Vol. 19 (Ancient Christian Writers). Westminister, (Md.): The Newman Press, 1954.

RAMSBOTHAN, H., ed. "The Commentary of Origen on the Epistle to the Romans." *The Journal of Theological Studies*, 13 (1912), p. 209–224, 357–368; and 14 (1913), p. 10–22: (Greek fragments).

ROBINSON, J. A. ed. *The Philocalia of Origen*. Cambridge: At the University Press, 1893.

SCHAFF, P. and WACE, H., eds. *The Nicene and Post-Nicene Fathers*. Vols. 3, 6. New York: The Christian Literature Co., 1893.

SCHERER, J. *Sources Chretiennes*. Vol. 67: *Origenes Dialecta cum Heraclida*. Text and French translation. Paris: Les Editions du Cerf, 1960.

_____. *Bibliotheque d'Etude*. Vol. 27: *Le Commentaire d'Origene Sur Rom. III. 5–V. 7*. Cairo: Institut Francais d'Archeologie Orientale, 1957.

STAHLIN, O. *Die Griechischen Christlichen Schriftseller der Ersten Drei Jahrhunderte*. Vol. 12, pts. 1–4: *Clement of Alexandria*. Leipzig: J. C. Hinrichs'sche Buchhandlung, 1905.

TOLLINTON R. B., trans. *Translation of Christian Literature*. Series I, Greek Texts: *Selections from the Commentaries and Homilies of Origen*. London: S. P. C. K., 1929.

Secondary Sources

ANDRESSEN, C. *Arbeiten zur Kirchengeschichte*. Bd. 30: *Logos und Nomos*. Berlin: Walter De Cruyter & Co., 1955.

BECK, G. *Das Werk Christi bei Origenes; zur Deutung Paulinischer Theologie im Turapapyrus des Romerbrief-Kommentars*. Bonn: Rhein. Friedr.-Wilh. Universitat, 1966.

BIGGS, C. *The Christian Platonists of Alexandria*. Oxford: Clarendon Press, 1913. Older work but still quite valuable as an introduction to Origen, his life, works and theology.

CADIOU, R. *Origen, His Life at Alexandria*. Trans. J. A. Southwell. London: B. Herder Book Co., 1944. A historical account of the philosophical trends prevalent in Alexandria at the beginning of the third century, and their influence on Origen's thought.

CHADWICK, H. "Origen, Celsus and the Stoa." *Journal of Theological Studies*, 48 (1947), 34–39.

_____. "Origen, Celsus and the Resurrection of the Body." *Harvard Theological Review*, 41 (1948), 83–102.

_____. "Rufinus and the Tura Papyrus of Origen's Commentary on Romans." *Journal of Theological Studies*, N.S. 10 (1959), 10–42.

_____. *Early Christian Thought and the Classical Tradition*. New York: Oxford University Press, 1966. A good summary study of Origen's thought and the environment that fostered it.

_____. "Origen." *The Cambridge History of Later Greek and Early Medieval Philosophy*. Part III., Chapt. 11. Cambridge: The University Press, 1967.

COPLESTON, F. *A History of Philosophy*. Vol. 1, pt. 2: *Greece and Rome*. Image Books. New York: Doubleday & Co., 1946.

CROUZEL, H. *Origene et la Connaissance Mystique*. Paris: Desclee De Brouwer, 1961.

CUMONT, FRANZ. *After Life in Roman Paganism*. New York: Dover Publications, Inc., 1959.

DANIELOU, J. *Origen*. Trans. W. Mitchell. New York: Sheed and Ward, 1955. An excellent text. Presents a total view of the complex nature of Origen's character and thought.

DE FAYE, E. *Origen and His Work*. Trans. F. Rothwell. New York: Columbia University Press, 1929. A study of Origen, his character and work from a philosophical viewpoint.

DE LUBAC, H. *Histoire et Espirit: L'intelligence de'l Ecriture d'apres Origene*. Paris: Aubier, 1950.

FAIRWEATHER, W. *Origen and Greek Patristic Theology*. Edinburgh: T. & T. Clark, 1901. A summary of Origen's works and their influence on later Greek theology.

HALTON, T. "The New Origen, Peri Pascha." *The Greek Orthodox Theological* Review, 28, 1 (1983), p. 73–80.

HANSON, R. P. C. *Allegory and Event*. Richmond: John Knox Press, 1959. This and the following are valuable studies of the sources and significance of Origen's interpretation of the Scriptures.

_____. *Origen's Doctrine of Tradition*. London: S. P. C. K., 1954.

HARNACK, A. *History of Dogma*. Trans. N. Buchanan. 3rd ed. Vols. 1, 2. New York: Dover Publication, Inc., 1961.

INGE, W. R. "Origen." *Proceedings of the British Academy*, 32 (1946), 123–145.

JACKSON, D. B. "Sources of Origen's Doctrine of Freedom." *Church History*, 35 (1966), 13–23.

KOCH, H. *Arbeiten zur Kirchengeschichte*. Bd. 22: *Pronoia und Paideusis; Studien uber Origenes und sein Verhältniszum Platonismus*. Berlin W. de Gruyter Co., 1932. A study of Origen's philosophy. Although one sided, treating Origen only as a philosopher, nonetheless quite valuable in understanding the philosophical side of Origen.

MUSURILLO, H. "The Recent Revival of Origen's Studies." *Theological Studies*, 24 (1963), 250–263.

_____. *The Fathers of the Primitive Church*. Mentor-Omega Books. New York: The New American Library, Inc., 1966.

OTIS, B. "Cappadocian Thought as a Coherent System." *Dumbarton Oaks Papers*, 12 (1958), 97–124.

OULTON, J. E. *The Library of Christian Classics*. Vol. 2: *Alexandrian Christianity*. Philadelphia: Westminister Press, 1954.

PATRICK, J. *The Apology of Origen in Reply to Celsus*. Edinburgh and London: Wm. Blackwood and Sons, 1892.

QUASTEN, J. Patrology. Vol. 2: *The Ante-Nicene Literature after Irenaeus*. Westminister, (Md.): The Newman Press, 1953.

SWETE, H. *An Introduction to the Old Testament in Greek*. New York: Ktav Publishing House, Inc., 1968. Excellent study of the development and organization of the Greek Old Testament. The section on the *Hexapla* is one of the best.

TAYLOR, C. "The Hexapla." *Dictionary of Christian Biography*. Vol. 3. Edited by W. Smith and H. Wace. New York: AMS Press, Inc., 1967.

TRIGG, J. W. *Origen: The Bible and Philosophy in the Third-century Church*. Atlanta: John Knox Press, 1983.

TRIPOLITIS, A. *The Doctrine of the Soul in the Thought of Plotinus and Origen*. New York: Libra Publishers, Inc., 1978.

VOLKER, W. *Das Vollkommenheitsideal des Origenes*. Tubingen: J. C. B. Mohr, 1931. A valuable study of Origen's mystical and ascetic language and thought.

WESTCOTT, B. F. "Origenes." *Dictionary of Christian Biography*. Vol. 4. Edited by W. Smith and H. Wace. New York: AMS Press, Inc., 1967. Good article although parts of it need updating in light of recent knowledge of Origen's works.

WOLFSON, H. A. *The Philosophy of the Church Fathers*. Vol. 1. Cambridge: Harvard Univ. Press, 1956.

_____. "Immortality of the Soul and Resurrection in the Philosophy of the Church Fathers." *Harvard Divinity Bulletin*, 22 (1956/57), 7–40.

_____. Philo. Vols. 1, 2. Cambridge, Mass.: Harvard Univ. Press, 1956.

YEOMANS, W. "The Spirituality of Origen." *The Month*, n.s. 20 (1958), 362–365.

148

Index